Buddhist Dream Yoga

Buddhist Dream Yoga

Dzogchen and the Practice of
Natural Light

CHÖGYAL NAMKHAI NORBU

edited and introduced by Michael Katz

SHAMBHALA

Shambhala Publications, Inc.
2129 13th Street
Boulder, Colorado 80302
www.shambhala.com

Cover art: CaoChunhai/iStock and ACALU Studio/Stocksy
Cover design: Daniel Urban-Brown

IPC-136EN00: Approved by the International Publications
Committee of the Dzogchen Community founded by
Chögyal Namkhai Norbu

9 8 7 6 5 4 3 2 1

Printed in the United States of America

Shambhala Publications makes every effort to print on
acid-free, recycled paper.

Shambhala Publications is distributed worldwide
by Penguin Random House, Inc., and its subsidiaries.

LIBRARY OF CONGRESS CATALOGING-IN-PUBLICATION DATA

Names: Namkhai Norbu, 1938–2018 author. | Katz, Michael, 1951– editor.
Title: Buddhist dream yoga: Dzogchen and the practice of natural light /
Chogyal Namkhai Norbu; edited and introduced by Michael Katz.
Description: Revised and enlarged edition. | Boulder: Shambhala Publications, 2025. |
Includes bibliographical references.
Identifiers: LCCN 2024003351 | ISBN 9781645472896 (trade paperback)
Subjects: LCSH: Rdzogs-chen. | Dreams—Religious aspects—Buddhism.
Classification: LCC BQ7662.4.N335 2025 | DDC 294.3/442—dc23/eng/20240511
LC record available at https://lccn.loc.gov/2024003351

Contents

Editor's Preface

It has been nearly a decade since the publication of the first edition of this book, which was titled *Dream Yoga and the Practice of Natural Light*. Recently, Chögyal Namkhai Norbu proposed that we enhance the original version with additional material from a profound and personal Dzogchen book that he has been writing for many years. It is a great honor and challenge to edit this material since no part of this pithy new manuscript has previously been made public.

Material pertinent to this book drawn from Chögyal Namkhai Norbu's manuscript has been translated by James Valby from the original Tibetan. This material expands and deepens the first edition's emphasis on specific exercises to develop awareness within the dream and sleep states. Within the manuscript, Chögyal Namkhai Norbu has included specific methods for training, transforming, dissolving, disordering, stabilizing, essentializing, holding, and reversing dreams. In addition, he has presented practices for maintaining one's practice throughout all moments of the day and night. The revision also includes a practice to develop the illusory body, profound clear light practices for developing contemplation, and methods for transference of consciousness at the time of death. The original edition of this book is currently available in more than ten languages. Over the years, tens of thousands have read the book and been inspired by Chögyal Namkhai Norbu's example and encouragement. Many have understood Rinpoche's message about the importance of using the time spent asleep and dreaming for spiritual or transpersonal purposes. Those of you reading this book for the first time will no doubt also be inspired, particularly since the second edition includes profound new material. Still, the habitual tendencies toward ignorance accrued over countless lifetimes are powerful. How many of us upon revisiting this text years later will see the signs of age in the mirror and not have much in the way of dream awareness to show for it? Whether or not you have read this book, it is likely that you, like myself, were unconscious in your dreams for most of the three years you have spent sleeping in the past decade.

Perhaps for you, like me, the decade has had its share of milestone events. As my infant son sleeps, I look into his peaceful face, and watch his eyelids flicker. My heart is filled with love and a desire to provide security, and I wonder if his dreams are of a previous life. These feelings and his presence, ironically, make me feel much closer to the *bardos* related to the transition we have come to call death.

According to the masters, progress in the practices of dream yoga and the Dzogchen practice of natural light will allow us to realize a form of enlightenment as we become lucid and aware during the moments of sleep. Conversely, continued ignorance within the states of sleep and dreaming will ensure only continued rebirth within one of the realms of samsara.

One of the important messages of this book is the distinction between the Dzogchen awareness referred to as *rigpa*, which arises from the practice of natural light, and the more relative but still important experience of lucidity. The lucidity experience, which may arise as a by-product of *rigpa* awareness or spontaneously due to karmic causes, assists in understanding the unreality of phenomena, which otherwise, during dream or the death experience, might be overwhelming. In the same way, we believe a nightmare to be real, but if we were to watch a similar scene within a movie, we would not necessarily be frightened.

Great yogis who have mastered Dzogchen awareness meditation are able to liberate themselves directly into the great clear
light at the moment of death. Practitioners who have at least
developed the capacity for occasional lucid dreaming may still
recognize the apparitions that arise within the *sidpai bardo* as
illusory. Reportedly, at the time of death when the mental body is
uncoupled from the physical body, all experiences are magnified
by a factor of seven. At these moments, according to our teachers,
there is still a possibility to achieve a form of liberation.

Even a few experiences of lucidity or, more ideally, seizing upon
the lucid Dream State as an opportunity to practice meditation
may lead to great opportunity. Alternatively, those who fail to recognize the illusory nature of the hallucinatory visions are appar-
ently blown by karmically induced waves of desire and fear until
they are reborn in one of the forms within cyclic existence.

One should be heartened by the advanced practices described
within this book. Although progress may not always be swift, it
is essential that all of us look carefully at our capacity and move
forward. This may entail making an effort to remember a dream
for the first time or, if more advanced, transforming dreams. There
are greater and greater gifts available to those who take up the
practice of dreamwork at any level.

Within my practice as a psychologist, I have had the opportunity to travel and conduct workshops in dreamwork over the
years. These workshops have relative aims often associated with
the goals of Western psychotherapy such as understanding the
unconscious and integrating that which is disowned. Additionally,
these workshops have assisted in my experience of developing
lucidity in dreams.

Occasionally when requested I have had to decline transmitting
the practice of natural light. This practice is linked with the transmission of Dzogchen, and only a master like Chögyal Namkhai
Norbu has the capacity to introduce this state of extraordinary
nonconceptual awareness. I hope that, if you have not already

done so, you will meet him and receive Dzogchen transmission directly from him.

The Buddha taught that every being possesses the capacity to recognize *rigpa*. Our obscurations cloud this awareness, which, according to one metaphor, continuously shines like the sun hidden by clouds. With practice, *rigpa* may be accessed at any moment, even within the various stages of sleep and dreaming. It is never destroyed.

There are myriad metaphors used to explain our lack of relationship with *rigpa*. One of my favorites is a story about a poor peasant who had nothing and continuously bemoaned his fate. Due to his extreme poverty, he was forced to use a stone for a pillow. The irony of the story is that the stone he used for his pillow was a diamond. Here this diamond represents *rigpa*.

I offer a more personal anecdote on the subject. Some years ago, I had seized an opportunity to conduct a retreat so as to interrupt my busy routine and focus on the inner life. On this occasion I had arranged to conduct a "dark retreat" according to instructions of Chögyal Namkhai Norbu. Contrary to expectations, the dark retreat affords a secure and tranquil environment to practice meditation without any external light.

The dark retreat, by virtue of reducing distractions to a minimum, provides a natural opportunity to practice dream yoga and the practice of natural light. Early on during what would be a twenty-two-day retreat in the dark, I had a dream. In it I was standing on a beach near the shoreline. In the surf I saw a crystal baby being washed back and forth by the waves. Although I had little hope that the baby was alive due to its prolonged exposure to the waves and the ocean, I nevertheless rushed down to the shore and snatched it out of the water. No sooner had I cradled it in my arms than the crystal baby became animated. Its uniqueness and beauty instantly struck me.

This dream expresses a great deal about our predicament—and its solution. Distracted by the 100,000 things of the world, our crystal awareness, or *rigpa*, is temporarily obscured by the waves of violent emotions. Despite this, it is never destroyed and, with attention, becomes alive.

It often takes a kind of shock to stir us from our complacency and habitual tendencies. In the same way that seeing a baby being thrown by the waves of violent surf would spur one to immediate action, this book is a reminder to awaken.

Michael Katz
New York City, 2001

Acknowledgments

The editor would like to acknowledge and remember the great Dzogchen teachers Dudjom Rinpoche, Dilgo Khyentse Rinpoche, Tulku Orgyen Rinpoche, Nyoshul Kyen Rinpoche, and Lama Gompo Tseden Rinpoche, who have left their bodies and returned to the Dharmakaya. May their work and aspirations be fulfilled!

The editor also would especially like to thank the following individuals for their assistance in completing this project.

The Venerable Khenpo Palden Rinpoche, for his assistance in translating the Mipham text *The Buddha No Farther Than One's Palm*. Khen Rinpoche is a meditation master and renowned scholar within the Nyingma order of Tibetan Buddhism. He offered invaluable insights into the meaning of the text and on many occasions took time from his busy schedule in order to complete the translation.

Khenpo Tsewong Dongyal for his assistance in translating the Mipham text. Khenpo Tsewong, a scholar, poet, and friend, has for many years shared his extensive knowledge and insights on dreams with the editor.

Lopon Tenzin Namdak for his advice and commentary pertaining to information contained in the introduction. A meditation master and guide of the Bön sect of Tibetan Dharma, Lopon Tenzin Namdak has worked ceaselessly to preserve the cultural and spiritual treasures of the Bönpo Tibetans.

Adriano Clemente for his editorial assistance.

James Valby for his assistance in translating material from Chögyal Namkhai Norbu's personal book for the second edition.

The editors at Snow Lion—Christi Cox, Jeff Cox, and Thomas Spiegelberg—for their invaluable editorial assistance and advice.

John Myrdhin Reynolds for his thoughtful contributions to the footnotes and for his research on Chögyal Namkhai Norbu's biography. John is the editor and translator of Chögyal Namkhai Norbu's text *The Cycle of Day and Night*, as well as the authoritative retranslation of *The Tibetan Book of the Great Liberation*.

Deborah Lockwood for her central assistance in translating the aforementioned Mipham text.

Susanna Green for her valuable research assistance.

Ester Lokos for her unfailing energy in manuscript preparation.

Representatives of the Dzogchen Community Lauri Denyer and Jo Shane for their valuable advice.

In addition, we would also like to thank the following friends for their help: Tsultrim Allione, Jill Baroff, Laura Baum, Mykl Castro, Cyril Christo, Stephanie Forest, Jan Green, Sherri Handlin, Sarah K. Huber, Oliver Leick, Sandy Litchfield, Maureen O'Brien, Leeana Pedron, John Shane, Gerry Steinberg, Marianna Swolo, and members of the Dzogchen Community who originally helped with translation and preparation of manuscripts.

Editor's Introduction

On a dark night in the 1950s, I raced from my bed and huddled at the door to my parents' room, frightened and still half asleep. I was perhaps five years old, and the vivid imagery of a nightmare was still fresh. It seemed real enough: a snake coiled in my bed— and my parents' reassurances that it was just a dream were little consolation.

This is one of my earliest dream memories. It was a dream that repeated again and again throughout childhood, adolescence, and even occasionally now as I move to middle age. What is a dream? Is there a special significance to a dream about snakes that repeats itself? Might snakes be messengers of the unconscious or possibly the early sexual stirrings of a child, or then again, a communication from another class of beings called *nagas* (snake-like beings who live in the water)? Perhaps the dream can only be understood within the context of the life of the dreamer, and thus have a specific personal meaning.

Archetypal material, personal anxieties and concerns, foretelling of the future, and communication with other dimensions of beings are all possibilities within dream according to the masters of dreamwork. Nevertheless, this statement should be qualified by saying that few encounter this range of dream experience. For most, dreaming is simply a rehashing of the impressions of the day within the context of the dreamer's wishes, fears, and personality.

In the 1950s, despite the presence of a few philosophers and contemporary thinkers for whom dreaming held renewed interest, most Americans, myself included, viewed dreams as having little significance. This blithe state of affairs was soon changed by the upheaval of the sixties. From the crucible of collective and personal crises resulting from the dramas of the decade, and concurrent with the popularity of yoga and various meditation forms, the awareness of dreams began to reassert itself in the general culture and in myself.

My memories of dreams from early childhood to college are little more than a blur. The vivid imagery and sharp recollections of childhood faded into fleeting images or no memory at all. But in 1978, my experience and understanding of the dream condition was radically transformed. I traveled to France to study with a renowned Tibetan lama, Dudjom Rinpoche. Among the topics he taught was dream yoga. Rinpoche spoke clearly about the need to strive for awareness even within the sleeping state. He compared the current sleeping state of humankind with the unconscious sleep of an animal. He lamented the waste of such a precious opportunity for developing oneself. I left the tent where the teachings were conducted in a strange state. All that I saw or heard seemed dreamlike, no doubt due to the great lama's powerful transmission. This unfamiliar perception lasted the entire day and into the evening. That night was unusual also. When I prepared to go to sleep, I resolved to follow Rinpoche's instructions for developing awareness and prayed for his assistance.

I fell asleep, but soon became aware that I was sleeping. I lay in a conscious luminous state. It was my first conscious experience of yogic sleep and the natural light of the mind.

Due to my own mind's obscurations, I did not make great progress in the practice of dream yoga and the practice of natural light. In fact, were it not for the one experience I had had, I probably would have relegated the whole topic to the realm of yogic feats, beyond the capacity of ordinary people. It was some years later, during a twenty-one-day solitary retreat, that I had another experience with yogic dreaming that was exciting and transformative. After two weeks had elapsed, my retreat had deepened considerably. Each night I followed Dudjom Rinpoche's instructions for developing the capacity for dream yoga. The intensive meditation practice extended to ten hours a day, and my mind became stronger. I was fascinated to be able to remember as many as eight dreams a night. On this particular night, I suddenly had the realization that I was both asleep and aware that I was dreaming. At the instant of the realization, the colors of the dreamscape became startlingly vivid and intense. I found myself standing on a cliff and looking out over a vast and beautiful valley. I felt relaxed and thrilled, and I reminded myself it was only a dream.

I looked out over the lovely vista for a short time and then resolved to go a step further, literally and figuratively. If it was truly a dream then there would be no reason why I couldn't fly. I leapt into space but, instead of flying, I found the dream transforming once again. Still lucid, my awareness appeared to be on a stairway. My body was no longer in the dream, but I was moving up the stairs. I had gone up one step and was making my way up another when the dream changed again. This time it was just black with no imagery whatsoever. I resisted the impulse to open my eyes. In truth, I was uncertain what to do, but I wished and willed the imagery to return and then suddenly I was back on the stairway. This recurrence of the stairway imagery lasted only momentarily and then I awoke.

The whole experience had been fascinating. I still consider it one of the most meaningful experiences of my life. The lama who supervised the retreat likened my experience to having passed a driving test. Subsequently, I have had many lucid experiences during dream. I can't say that they occur each night, but they do occur regularly. Their frequency increases during times when I practice meditation intensively, such as in retreat. Also, if I awaken and practice meditation during the night, I find that I frequently have lucid dreams upon returning to sleep.

Over the course of time, I have also had dreams that were psychic in nature. For example, while on retreat, I dreamt of my lover. Although I was not lucid during the dream, my recollection was clear. Her image appeared. She was luminous, radiant, and yet she was sobbing. The next day, I had plans to pick her up at a train station in upstate New York. To test my dream experience, I told her that I was very sorry she had been distraught the previous night. Her look of surprise told me instantly that the dream was accurate. She told me that she had been ill and had indeed cried bitterly.

As I mentioned, it seemed clear that these experiences increased when I had the opportunity to practice meditation or the dream yoga instructions intensively. It was during such a period that I joined Chögyal Namkhai Norbu for a seminar in Washington, D.C. He had been traveling with one of his oldest students, and she had become seriously ill. In my dream, I found myself with Chögyal Namkhai Norbu; he was very preoccupied with the student's health crisis. I said, "Rinpoche, she's dying." Rinpoche replied, "No, I've treated her, and she's getting better." The next day the good news was that she was indeed recovering, but even more startling was Chögyal Namkhai Norbu's awareness of our dream conversation before I told him about it. Later I had other dreams where Chögyal Namkhai Norbu was talking with me, and occasionally I would also say something intelligent in return. Chögyal Namkhai Norbu would take great interest in these experiences, and sometimes the next day would ask me if I had had an interesting dream the previous night. Occasionally, he would ask me, and if I only vaguely remembered, he would say, "You must, you must try to remember." Not long ago I visited my parents' house. They have lived there for my entire life. I slept in the same room where I slept as a child. As I slept, I had a dream that there was a snake in the bed with me. Rather than threatening me, it seemed to want to cuddle like a pet. Although I was not completely lucid, I recall wondering what to do with this friendly though clearly uninvited snake. Upon awakening, I thought about this dream and its meaning at some length. Perhaps I had become more comfortable with that which was once fearful. Then again I remembered Chögyal Namkhai Norbu's comment that with increased clarity, dreams might come to be something like a United Nations conference. Might the dream snake have been a "delegate"? For it is Chögyal Namkhai Norbu's contention that there are many classes of beings with whom it is possible to communicate within the Dream State.

Countless theories have been developed to account for the universally shared set of experiences we call dreaming. Although these theories may differ radically regarding the origin and significance of dreams, there is widespread agreement that many dreams are mysterious, powerful, and creative.

Dreams have held a central place in many societies. In many cultures the importance of dreaming was taken for granted, and the ability to remember or even consciously alter a dream was nurtured. Dreams have figured prominently—sometimes centrally—in religions, assisted on the hunt, inspired sacred patterns for arts and crafts, and provided guidance in times of war, crisis, or illness. The dreamer of a "big dream" was frequently referred to as a priest or priestess, a title earned by virtue of their having been blessed by the gods.

Ancient Egyptians and other traditional peoples systematically interpreted dreams for the purpose of deciphering messages from the gods. Egyptian priests called "masters of the secret things" were considered intermediaries. With the advent of writing, the knowledge of dream interpretation was recorded. An early book on dream interpretation, written in Egypt some two thousand years before the Common Era, is contained in what is now called the Chester Beatty Papyrus.

In many cultures, dreamers preparing to receive an important or healing dream participate in elaborate rituals. These rituals, widespread in early history, are especially well-documented in Native American societies as well as in Asia, ancient Babylon,

Greece, and Rome. Invocational, or "incubation," ceremonies would feature rituals guided by trained initiates and frequently took place in special temples built on important and beautiful sacred sites.

After making offerings to the gods or a sacrifice for purification, the dream seeker would sometimes drink potions to enhance the experience. Depending on the culture, the ingredients for these potions might include a variety of psychotropic drugs.[1] The sacred places were often selected through the esoteric science of geomancy or through a priest's psychic revelation. The site of these temples was particularly important to the ancient Greeks, for example, because their chthonic deities[2] were believed to reside in special locations.

All aspects of the temples themselves were designed to mobilize and heighten the workings of the unconscious mind as well as spirits. For example, in Greece, the cult of the oracle-god Asclepius[3] was symbolized by the snake, and dream seekers would often sleep in a place where snakes moved about freely. After the elaborate rituals, Asclepius frequently appeared to the dreamer as a bearded man or as an animal, and in many instances the individual would awaken cured. At the height of their popularity, these Asclepian centers for dream incubation numbered in the hundreds.

Instances of healing through rituals such as these are also widespread in contemporary shamanic cultures.[4] For example, Richard Grossinger, the author of numerous books on dream ethnography, cites Native American sources from among the Crow, Blackfoot, Kwakiutl, and Winnebago tribes recounting dreams in which an animal or bird, such as a snake or loon, appeared and taught cures, which, when applied in waking life, were found to have healing power.

Dreams have also inspired important scientific advances. Perhaps the most celebrated of these is the discovery of the molecular structure of benzene by August Kekule. His account:

My mind was elsewhere . . . I turned the chair to the fireplace, and fell half asleep. Again the atoms gamboled in front of my eyes. Smaller groups this time kept mostly in the background. My mind's eye, trained by repeated visions of the same sort, now distinguished larger formations of various shapes. Long chains . . . everything in movement, twisting and turning like snakes. And look what was that? One snake grabbed its own tail, and mockingly the shape whirled before my eyes. I awoke as if struck by lightning; this time again I spent the rest of the night working out its consequences.

The Russian chemist Dmitri Mendeleev discovered the periodic table method of classifying elements according to atomic weight while dreaming. Elias Howe completed his invention of the sewing machine while dreaming. Albert Einstein's theory of relativity came to him partly in a dream. Other dream-inspired creations include literary masterpieces such as Dante's *Divine Comedy*, Voltaire's *Candide*, "The Raven" by Poe, and *Ulysses* by James Joyce. Robert Louis Stevenson was able to formulate stories while dreaming; these he later wrote down and published. Even some popular music compositions by Billy Joel and Paul McCartney have come in dreams. Such unusual dreams notwithstanding, our society as a whole has lost touch with the art of dreaming. Recently, however, a widespread interest in the creative power of dreams has surfaced, emerging from several divergent disciplines, including science, Western depth psychology, the increasing awareness of native cultures, and religion.

Science and Dream Phenomena

The modern, scientific description of dream phenomena has followed upon the discovery in 1952 of Nathaniel Kleitman and his students that dreaming is accompanied by rapid eye movements

(R.E.M.). Other facts about dreaming have emerged through more recent experimentation. For example, we know that all people dream and that approximately 25 percent of sleep is dream time. Dreams are crucial for human health, dreaming is a right brain activity, and virtually all dreams are accompanied by R.E.M. Sleep has four stages, or depths, but dreaming occurs only in the first stage. We also know that we move through the four stages of sleep several times in a typical night, and consequently we normally dream many times each night. It has been observed that a person who is deprived of dream time will make up for it in subsequent nights. A greater percentage of sleeping time is spent dreaming as we approach dawn.

Let us focus on the phenomenon of lucid dreams, those unusual dreams in which the dreamer finds him or herself suddenly self-consciously aware, or "lucid," while dreaming. Once frequently dismissed, but now scientifically verified, reports of lucid dreaming have existed in literature for thousands of years. For example, Aristotle made the following statement: "For often when one is asleep, there is something in consciousness which declares that what presents itself is but a dream."[5]

In the early 1900s, a Dutch psychiatrist by the name of Frederik van Eeden studied this phenomenon in a systematic fashion and coined the term "lucid dreaming" to describe it. Before him, the Marquis d'Hervey de Saint Denys had investigated dream phenomena and published his findings in 1867 in the book *Dreams and How to Guide Them*. In this book, Saint Denys described his ability to awaken within his dreams as well as to direct them.

Stephen LaBerge, a modern researcher of dream phenomena, developed a methodology that utilizes the rapid eye movements that accompany dreaming to train lucidity.[6] In one study, subjects listened to a recording that repeated the phrase "this is a dream" every few seconds. This was played after the beginning of each R.E.M. period. He then asked his sleeping subjects to signal their lucidity by moving their eyes in a prearranged pattern. Approximately 20 percent of his subjects were able to achieve lucidity in their Dream States through this technique. By identifying the link between eye signaling and dream lucidity, LaBerge has gone on to develop techniques that enhance the rate of lucid dreaming by more than tenfold and techniques that stabilize lucid dreaming effectively. A major line of his research has been developing techniques and technology to make lucid dreaming more easily accessible. The "Model-A" of this emerging "oneirotechnology" is the NovaDreamer, a biofeedback device that gives cues during R.E.M. sleep reminding users that they are dreaming.

The following account, by a participant in a dream awareness seminar, serves to illustrate the phenomenon of being awake, or lucid, within a dream:

On Wednesday morning, January 13, 1988, I became aware that I was dreaming, and I decided that the best thing to do would be to fly in the sky. I hitched myself to a jet, and we went very high into the stratosphere. I then had the jet reverse course so I could hang from it and see the world. I looked down and saw the earth as a great sphere. Then I dropped my hold and stretched my arms out wide to glide better. I stayed quite high (literally and figuratively) in the sky, in order to realize the immensity and beauty of this vast ocean as seen from above.

After a short period, I glided down lower, very slowly, finding myself over a beautiful island. This island view was pleasing to me. It was early morning; quiet and even light allowed for clear sight of the still masts of the many yachts docked at the harbor. Beyond their tall poles and white decks, there stood hillside mountains with homes built right into them. It was a splendid and majestic sight, the yachts and mountains in clear, even morning light. It was reminiscent of a combination of two places I had been before. In Paxos, Greece, there are harbored many yachts, and Marin City, California, there are homes built into the hills. I continued to view this sight before I fell into a more general type of dreaming in which I didn't control the view or determine what I would like to do.

The preceding account is typical insofar as lucid dreams frequently include flying. On some occasions the dreamer is first aware that he or she is flying, and then suddenly becomes lucid. On other occasions the dreamer becomes lucid and subsequently tries to fly. Another common feature that this dreamer shares with other lucid dreamers is the sense of heightened color and emotion, the sense of participating in an awesome and magnificent experience. Not all lucid dreams are so expansive, however. Kenneth Kelzer, an author and lucid dreamer, comments upon the persistent theme of being within a jail that characterizes one series of lucid dreams he had. "The symbol of the jail cell in these three dreams provided me with an essential reminder that I am still a prisoner, still working to attain that fullness of mental freedom to which I aspire."[7]

Dreams and Depth Psychology

In the past century, the frenzied expansion of industrial technology occurred at a great price. For complex reasons it helped to spawn the great world wars. The wide-scale destruction and loss of life resulted in a questioning of values—especially those of a religious and moral nature. Against the specter of apocalypse, the despair of meaninglessness, and the perceived ruins of Western religious ceremony, contemporary thinkers sought to understand the workings of the psyche by studying less conscious phenomena such as fantasy and dream, thus developing the approach of depth psychology. Evoking and developing awareness of unconscious processes was perceived as valuable for healing the weary, confused soul.

Sigmund Freud, the founder of modern Western psychology, called dreamwork the "royal road to the unconscious," and helped reawaken interest in dreaming. Freud's seminal work, *The Interpretation of Dreams*, represented a radical departure from previous contemporary Western psychiatric theory. Freud asserted that dreams are symbolic representations of repressed wishes, most of which are sexual. Through the process of "wish fulfillment" the dreamer released the "excitement" of the impulse. He thought the dream would typically be organized in a disguised or symbolic way because these wishes, or impulses, were unacceptable.

Noting that a single dream might represent an enormous amount of personal material, Freud postulated that each character or element of the dream was a condensed symbol. The labyrinth of meaning might be unraveled through the process of free association. Techniques of listing all associations to a dream continue to be widely used among contemporary analysts. Less well recognized is Freud's acknowledgment of the existence of telepathy within the Dream State. This was published in his lectures on psychoanalysis in 1916.[8]

Carl Jung was perhaps the first Western psychologist to be interested in Buddhism[9] and Eastern religion. Jung, once a close student of Freud, later broke away from his mentor. Jung explained that he could not accept Freud's overwhelming emphasis on a sexual root for all repressions, nor his narrow, anti-religious views. Jung considered libido to be a universal psychic energy, whereas for Freud it was simply sexual energy.[10]

Jung also postulated the existence of a deep, encompassing, cultural memory accessible through powerful dreams. He labeled this memory the "collective unconscious" and considered it to be a rich and powerful repository of the collective memory of the human race.

Jung postulated that dreams generally compensate for the dreamer's imbalance in their waking life and bring that which is unconscious to consciousness. He noted that individuals function with certain characteristic styles, for example with feeling or intellect, and in an introverted or extroverted manner. If a person were primarily intellectual and their feeling side largely suppressed or unconscious, strong feelings might then manifest more frequently in their dream life. A feeling type, conversely, might have intellectual dreams in order to compensate for the dominant conscious attitude.

Fritz Perls, the founder of the Gestalt school of psychology, proclaimed dreams to be the "royal road to integration." For Perls, dreaming and the awareness of dreaming were essential for one's coming into balance and owning all the parts of one's personality. He based his dreamwork on the supposition that facets of a dream might all be perceived as projections of parts or personas of the dreamer. Perls's contribution to dreamwork and therapy was his keen awareness that neurotic functioning is caused by disowning parts of oneself. He suggests that we disown or alienate ourselves by projection and repression. We may reclaim these unacknowledged aspects of our personalities by enacting or dramatizing parts of a dream. Through this process we recognize more fully our own attitudes, fears, and wishes, thus allowing our individualization and maturation process to proceed unimpeded.

The following dramatic example of one woman's enactment of a dream part in the style of Gestalt therapy will illustrate Perls's technique of dreamwork. The woman recounted a dream in which a small aerosol spray can was one of many items on a dresser bureau, and she dramatized the different items in turn. When she reached the spray can, she announced, "I'm under enormous pressure. I feel as if I'm about to explode." The enactment of this dream provided swift and clear feedback regarding an unresolved issue in her life.

Another school of contemporary psychology that respects the dream experience is represented by Medard Boss. Boss considers the dream to be a reality that should be understood as an autobiographical episode. In the process of understanding one's dreams, Boss would encourage the dreamer to actually experience and dwell within that unique moment.

Not all psychologists acknowledge the great potential in advanced dreamwork. For example, in the phenomenological school as articulated by Boss and Keny, dreams are considered to constitute a "dimmed and restricted world view," and are "privative, deficient, and constricted in comparison with waking." The object relations school as typified by Ronald Fairbairn considers dreams to be schizoid phenomena, cauldrons of anxieties, wishes, and attitudes.

Certain current scientific theories have also gone further in denying a basic, meaningful, organizing principle within the state of dreaming. J. Allen Hobson of Harvard Medical School proposes in his book, *The Dreaming Brain*, a "dream state generator" located within the brain stem. The generator, when engaged, fires neurons randomly and the brain attempts to make sense of these weak signals by organizing them into the dream story. Others have proposed similarly mechanistic explanations of dream phenomena. Francis Crick and Graeme Mitchison suggest that dreams occur to unlearn useless information. Connections that are unimportant and temporarily stored are thus discharged and forgotten.

Alternate theories by Carl Sagan and others that attempt to account for the most famous creative acts that have arisen within the Dream State have proposed that such dreams result from uninhibited right brain activity. According to this theory, the left brain, which is usually dominant during the day, is suppressed during dreams. Consequently, the right brain is less inhibited and can become spectacularly intuitive and creative. This theory would account, for example, for Kekule's discovery of the benzene molecule as an example of the right brain's skill at pattern recognition in contrast to the more analytic activity of the left brain. This theory, although interesting, cannot account for all types of telepathic and creative dreams.

John Grant, a specialist in dream research, recently spent considerable effort in providing explanations for dream telepathy. His conclusion after much effort in debunking sensational claims was that only 95 percent of dream telepathy and dreams that predict future events might be explicable according to known laws and science. His subjective statistic and inability to account for the other 5 percent of unusual dreams that anticipate the future fits in well with Chögyal Namkhai Norbu's theory of dream phenomena. This theory acknowledges both common dreams whose origins are our wishes and anxieties, as well as creative clarity type dreams that arise out of awareness.

Many analytic and scientific approaches still contend that the content of all dreams is merely chaotic or symbolic and composed of a cauldron of anxieties, wishes, and attitudes. Consequently, contemporary Western dreamworkers do not generally recognize or understand the possibilities for dreamwork assumed in traditional societies. While Western depth psychology works with dreams as an approach to individual mental health, its understanding of the possibilities for dreamwork, though improving, is still limited. The range of these other possibilities and the need for determining priorities appear when we explore dreamwork systems evolved in other cultures.

Dreamwork in Traditional Cultures

Systems for dreamwork and dream awareness have been found for millennia within Buddhism, Taoism, Hinduism, Sufism, and other traditional cultures throughout the world.[11] These dreamwork systems were and are often cloaked in secrecy and reserved for the initiate. The recorded dream experiences of traditional peoples whose cultures are still relatively intact may help expand our understanding of the possibilities of dreamwork and dream awareness, including the phenomena of lucidity, telepathy, and precognitive dreams. The Australian Aborigines believe in the existence of ancestral beings who are more powerful than most humans and are considered to have other-than-human physical counterparts such as rocks, trees, or land formations. According to the authors of a comprehensive book on Aboriginal culture, *Dreamings: The Art of Aboriginal Australia*, edited by Peter Sutton, the spiritual dimension in which these beings have their existence is described as the "Dreamtime." The ancestors, known as "Dreamings," may be contacted through dreams, though they are not considered to be a product of dreams. This underscores the Aboriginal belief in multiple classes of beings and alternate dimensions within which other classes of beings reside.

Noteworthy are the Aboriginal beliefs regarding texts, art, and songs that come in dreams. A new song, story, design, or other creative product received in a dream is perceived by the Aboriginal peoples as a reproduction of an original creation rendered by an ancestor. These artistic gifts are considered to be channeled rather than original creations. Within the tribe, the dreamer is revered as a conduit through which the wisdom of the ancestors is received, not as the originator of this wisdom. According to the myths and dream records of contemporary Aboriginal peoples, artistic products have come in dreams since time immemorial and continue to enrich Aboriginal culture today.

The Senoi people of what is today called Malaysia ostensibly provided a documented instance of a traditional people who placed an unusually high value on creative dreamwork. Patricia Garfield in her book *Creative Dreaming* presents dream techniques attributed to the Senoi by anthropologist Kilton Stewart. According to Stewart, the Senoi focused an unusual amount of attention on dreamwork and developed sophisticated methods for influencing and deriving creative inspiration from dreams through reinforcement, self-suggestion, and daily discussion of their dreams. Dr. Garfield summarized the key Senoi dreamwork goals as follows: confronting and overcoming danger within a dream, accepting and moving toward pleasurable experiences within the dream, and making the dream have a positive or creative outcome. The integrative effects of this work may very well be a cause for a lowered frequency of mental disorder. However, later researchers did not substantiate Stewart's claim that Senoi society approached a utopian ideal.[12]

Presumably the Senoi had strong motivation for developing control of their dreams because of the great premium their tribe placed on these abilities. Contemporary researchers report that the ability to influence dreams toward positive outcomes seems to have effects such as increased self-confidence and creativity.

The creative potential of dreams is unquestionably valued in traditional Tibetan culture. Within Tibetan Buddhism there is a class of literature called *milam gyi terdzöd*, or "dream treasures." These treasures are teachings that are considered to be the creations of enlightened beings. The teachings were purposefully hidden or stored in order to benefit future generations. As a demonstration of their wisdom, the originators of these treasures often prophesied the name of their discoverer and the time of discovery.

Buddhist and Bönpo[13] systems for dream awareness training appear to be thousands of years old.[14] In the interview presented in this book, Chögyal Namkhai Norbu comments that dream awareness training was discussed extensively in the text of the inconceivably ancient *Mahamaya Tantra*. Khenpo Palden Sherab, a renowned Buddhist scholar, agrees that the tantras are inconceivably ancient. According to Khenpo, many millennia before the historical Buddha Shakyamuni lived, the tantras were taught by the buddhas of past eras to both human and nonhuman beings.

Consider, for example, the extraordinary dream experience Chögyal Namkhai Norbu had while on retreat in Massachusetts in the summer of 1990. Night after night, a woman whom Rinpoche considered to be a dakini[15] appeared in his dream and taught him a complex series of dances with intricate steps for up to thirty-six dancers. Day after day, Rinpoche transcribed the lessons from the dreams of the night before. He also taught a group of his students parts of this dance, which accompany a special song for deepening meditation. The tune itself had been received in another dream years earlier as related in dream number one in Chapter Six. Having heard firsthand accounts of these dreams, and having participated in this exquisite dance, I can only say that Rinpoche's experience is profound beyond words.

Shortly after Rinpoche's retreat, he was visited by a Native American teacher who goes by the name of Thunder. Thunder is the descendant of a long lineage of Native American medicine men and healers. After hearing accounts of Rinpoche's dance and examining photos of our attempts to learn it, she noted its similarity to the Native American Ghost Dance.

The following series of dreams related by Chögyal Namkhai Norbu may serve to illustrate the human potential within the Dream State as awareness develops.

In 1959, I had already fled Tibet to the country of Sikkim. The situation within Tibet was deteriorating rapidly. As the news of killings and destruction reached us, I became increasingly worried about the members of my family who remained in Tibet. Many of us prayed to Tara asking for her help. It was during this period that I had the following dream:

I was walking through a mountainous area. I remember the beautiful trees and flowers. Near the road on which I was traveling there were wild animals, but they were peaceful and gentle to me. I was aware that I was en route to Tara's temple located on a mountain ahead. I arrived at a place near the temple where there was a small field with many trees and red flowers. There was also a young girl approximately eleven or twelve years old.

When the young girl saw me, she immediately gave me a red flower and inquired where I was going. I replied, "I am going to the temple of Tara in order to pray for Tibet." In response she said, "There is no need for you to go to the temple; just say this prayer." She then repeated a prayer to me many times that began, "Om Jetsumma . . ." I began to say this prayer, repeating it as I was holding the flower. I repeated the prayer again and again. I actually woke myself up by saying this prayer so loudly.

Some years later I had a related dream. In this dream, I again found myself in the field that marked the approach to the temple of Tara. It was the same as the previous dream, but there was no young girl. I looked ahead of me and there was the temple at the top of a mountain. I continued my journey until I arrived. It was a simple temple, not elegantly designed or decorated. It was open to the east.

I entered and noticed that upon the wall was a painting of the *shitro* mandala of the one hundred peaceful and wrathful deities. On bookshelves there were many Tibetan books, including the *Tengyur* and *Kangyur*. I was looking over the collection when I noticed a Tibetan man at the door. He was dressed somewhat like a lama, but not completely. He asked me, "Did you see the speaking Tara?"

I replied that I had not yet seen the speaking Tara, but that I would like to. The man then led me to a room with statues. As he turned toward the door to leave, he said, "There is the speaking Tara." I didn't see anything at first, but then I noticed that the man was looking upward to the top of a column. I followed his gaze, and there at the top of the column was a statue of Green Tara. She was represented as a child of perhaps seven or eight years. It was a nice statue, but I didn't hear it speak, and subsequently I awakened.

The next chapter in this story was not a dream at all. In 1984, I was traveling in northern Nepal, heading toward Tolu Monastery, when I recognized the field where in my dream the girl had given me the flower and prayer. I looked ahead and there was the temple. When I arrived, everything was exactly the same as in my dream. I walked over to the column and looked for the "speaking Tara." It wasn't there. That was the only detail that differed. Not too long ago, I heard that one of my students had presented the temple with a statue of Green Tara, which they placed on top of the column as a sort of commemoration. If you travel to that temple today, you can see it there.

Developing Dream Awareness

The possibility of developing awareness within the Dream State, and of subsequently having intensely inspiring experiences as well as the ability to control dreams, is well documented. It is the pathway to higher-order dreaming made possible by the practices outlined later in this book.[16] Cross-cultural parallels point very strongly to the existence of a class of dream experiences that have fueled the advance of humankind's cultural and religious progress. These dreams, which Chögyal Namkhai Norbu refers to as clarity dreams, seem to arise out of intense mental concentration upon a particular problem or subject, as well as through meditation and ritual. Startling, creative, or transcendent outcomes often emerge from these special dreams, some of which may be channeled.

In a dream awareness seminar I conducted in 1989, a participant recounted the following dream: "When I was a young child I used to have a recurring dream of being threatened by an old, ugly dwarf who was terrifying to me. Each time he would appear, I would either run away in that nightmarish manner of not seeming to get anywhere, or pretend to faint just to get away from him. Finally, during one dream, I became very annoyed and decided I was tired of being threatened. I turned on him and told him he was just part of my dream. When I did that, I wasn't frightened of him anymore. The dream never recurred after that."

Even my own relatively minor dream experiences have occasionally seemed to support the possibility of dreams that predict the future. For example, last year I attended a sporting event with two friends. I was impressed by the colorful stadium. That night I dreamt of a baseball player. His picture was on the front page of a newspaper. I tried to read and remember the print. By the next morning, I only recalled the name Clark. Upon awakening, I purchased the *New York Times*, as is my habit, and discovered a photograph of Will Clark, a baseball player, on the front page. Perhaps you might argue that this was coincidental. If so, you would be making the same argument that Aristotle used in order to counter Heraclitus, who believed in precognitive dreaming (just to illustrate how long the controversy has raged). Regardless of whether my dream about Will Clark was truly prophetic, I personally have come to believe that within the higher order, creative class, of dreams, there is a category predictive of the future.

If this is actually the case, it would suggest that the future is somehow available in the present. Within Tibetan Buddhist, Bönpo, and other traditions, enlightened beings are considered to have the capacity to see the past, present, and future.

If there is indeed significant evidence of a class of higher-order dreams, questions arise concerning how one may develop the capacity to experience them and whether or not there are reasons (beyond their ability to increase creativity) to cultivate this capacity. According to the Tibetan Dzogchen tradition, the key to working with dreams is the development of greater awareness within the Dream State. Chögyal Namkhai Norbu discusses this awareness in his chapter on the practice of natural light.

Over the course of a typical night, as much as eight hours may be spent sleeping, of which two or more hours might be spent dreaming. Are we able to remember dreams from each of these sessions? How precisely do we remember their details? An individual with no awareness of dreams, who is largely unable to remember them, has sacrificed an awareness of a large portion of her or his life. This person is missing the opportunity both to explore the rich and fertile depths of the psyche as well as to grow spiritually. Consider the message of this Buddhist verse:

When the state of dreaming has dawned,
Do not lie in ignorance like a corpse.

Enter the natural sphere of unwavering attentiveness.
Recognize your dreams and transform illusion into luminosity.
Do not sleep like an animal.
Do the practice which mixes sleep and reality.

There is no doubt that lucid dreams and clarity experiences are fascinating occurrences, which seemingly have positive benefits for self-esteem, integration of personality, and overcoming of fear. It is critical to place their occurrence within the context of the quest for spiritual transformation or enlightenment. Insofar as a culture such as ours tends to value experience for experience's sake, there is the danger of missing the forest for the trees.

One lama from the Tibetan Buddhist tradition likened the pursuit of lucid dream experience to mere play and games except when it arises as the by-product of an individual's development of meditative clarity through the Dzogchen night practice of the white light or Tantric dream yoga. Although there does seem to be relative value in lucid dream experience, from the Buddhist perspective its usefulness is limited unless the individual knows how to apply the lucid awareness in the after-death states of the *chönyid* and *sidpai bardos*.

In the Dzogchen teaching, which for millennia has recognized lucid dream experiences as well as such parapsychological phenomena as telepathy and precognition, the student is constantly advised that "one must not be attached to experience." This counters the Western trend to value experience for its own sake. Western approaches also encourage a systematic analysis of the content of dreams, whereas Dzogchen teachers encourage practitioners not to dwell upon dream phenomena.

Although there seem to be clear benefits from the extensive examination of dream material, it is quite possible that these benefits are only for the beginner. For the advanced practitioner, awareness itself may ultimately be far more valuable than the experience and content, no matter how creative. Great teachers have reported that dreams cease completely when awareness becomes absolute, to be replaced by luminous clarity of an indescribable nature.

The presentation of techniques for dreamwork from these ancient traditions is important because these traditions are in danger of extinction. Although there have been many books written on the general topic of dreams, at the time that the first edition of this book was published there had been relatively little that would serve to bring dreamwork into the spiritual context. Buddhist, Bönpo, and Taoist teachers have acknowledged that this situation has influenced their decisions to teach more openly, and subsequently, in the past decade, esteemed teachers such as the Dalai Lama, Tenzin Wangyal, and Gyatrul Rinpoche have published books on the subject of dreamwork that serve to enhance the information and techniques found in *Buddhist Dream Yoga*.

In a personal way, this project served to focus my attention on the power and richness of maintaining awareness during the often neglected sleep time. Regardless of our material circumstances, if we cultivate this capacity, we possess a wish-fulfilling jewel. In the West, the scientific exploration of sleep and dreams is quite new, but within the larger community of humankind, the arcane science of dream awareness and exploration has been cherished for millennia. Pioneer psychologists of the twentieth century have commented upon dream phenomena. Sigmund Freud called dreams "the royal road to the unconscious," and Fritz Perls called them the "royal road to integration." In their way, these assertions may be true, but they are overshadowed by the possibility that the awareness of dreams is a path to enlightenment.

I am grateful for the opportunity to help chronicle the extraordinary dream experiences and teachings on the Dream State of Dzogchen master Chögyal Namkhai Norbu.

Michael Katz
New York City, 2001

Buddhist Dream Yoga

CHAPTER 1

The Nature and Classes of Dreams

In a sutra, Buddha Shakyamuni[1] describes the phenomenal world that we generally consider to be real through the use of multiple metaphors. He likens our reality to a shooting star, an optical illusion, a flickering butter lamp, dew drops at dawn, bubbles in water, lightning, a dream, and clouds. According to the Buddha, all aggregated existence, all dharmas,[2] and in fact all phenomena are actually unreal and constantly changing like these examples.

Another sutra employs additional poetic metaphors to show the essential unreal nature of our condition. These include the reflection of the moon in water, a mirage, a city composed of sounds, a rainbow, a reflection in a mirror, and also a dream.

The example of a dream is included in these sutras because we all know that if we examine a dream, we will not find anything concrete. Even though the primary and secondary causes for its arisal may be discovered, still there is nothing actually concrete or real about the dream itself.

Although there are many different conditions that may lead to dreaming, the product of the conditions, our dreams, may in general be grouped into two main categories: the more common types of dreams arising from karmic traces[3] and other types of dreams arising due to the clarity of mind.

Within the category of dreams that are caused by karma, there are dreams that are mainly related to the three states of existence, i.e., the body, energy (or speech), and the tensions of the mind of the individual; and there is another class that is related to karmic traces. The latter has three causes, namely, traces of karma originating in a past life, in youth, and in the recent past of the individual.

In the tradition of Tibetan medicine, a physician who is conducting an investigation as to the origin of an illness will also consider to which of the three existences the sick person's dreams relate. With this information, he or she can discover the real condition and situation of the body, energy, and mind of the sick person. Sometimes an individual who has a serious illness that is difficult to cure may be in that condition due to karmic causes originating in youth or even in a past life. It may also happen that the illness is the result of a karmic cause due to recent actions. Thus, examining dreams becomes one of the most important means for analyzing and discovering the principal and secondary causes of the problem.

What is meant by dreams related to the individual's three existences? These dreams arise due to any kind of experience of the body, speech, or mind. Thus, experiences directly related to the individual's elements, energy, and emotions may become instantaneous causes for manifesting some dream experience, either good, bad, or neutral.

For example, a person who is sleeping on a bed in an awkward position may be uncomfortable or in pain. The disturbance may become the instant cause for a negative dream. Or, if a person is not sleeping well due to obstructed breathing, dreams of suffocating or being strangled may arise. Further, it is not difficult to understand that feelings such as joy or sadness associated with the mind may also be the instant secondary cause of having dreams. These are examples of dreams related to conditions of the individual's three existences.

Within the category of dreams that are caused by karma, one

type encompasses those whose cause originates in a previous life. In this kind of dream, unfamiliar things may appear that the person has not experienced in this life, such as visions of another country or strange peoples who have unfamiliar customs or language. These dreams may repeat so often that the dreamer becomes knowledgeable of the once unfamiliar world. Such experiences suggest the existence of a very strong habit from a past life that has left a karmic trace in the individual. Or a dream may appear of an unusual country in which there is a strange person who wants to trouble or kill the dreamer; as a result, the dreamer has a very strong feeling of fear. This sometimes means that a similar situation occurred in a previous life—the person's conditions were affected strongly enough to leave a karmic trace. This trace reappears when the secondary conditions are ripe. As another example of this type of karmic dream, if someone murdered me in a past life, I may still in this life have dreams of being murdered. It is not true that what we dream is always about our experiences from this life. If an event is very weighty, then you may feel it life after life. When you sleep very deeply, you may create a perfect potential for past karma to manifest within your dreams.

If you merely have heavy tension, it may also repeat in your dreams. For example, when you are a child and someone makes a problem for you, it could repeat in your dreams. Or if today I have a problem with someone, it may repeat tonight in my dream. The principle is that if you have heavy tension and you sleep deeply, the tension tends to repeat. This is one kind of dream, a karmic dream of *pagchag*. *Pagchag* means traces of something left. For example, if there is an empty bottle that once contained perfume, you can still smell the trace of perfume. That is *pagchag*. This first type of karmic dream does occur, even though it is not experienced frequently by all people.

Karmic dreams of the second type are those whose causes were developed in the dreamer's youth. If the youthful person was frightened or involved in an accident, that experience may leave a trace, and thus dreams may occur later in life that relate to the event either literally or thematically. Or if, for example, as a child, someone experienced an earthquake that produced great fear, then later in life there is the potential that the trace might become activated with the proper secondary causes, such as the experience of another earthquake.

The third type of karmic dream includes dreams originating from recent actions that touched the person deeply. The person might have been extremely angry recently and, as a consequence, may have fought with someone. That intense anger leaves a trace. Because of this, a dream arises that is similar in situation or theme.

The causes of these three types of dreams are principally karmic, that is, related to an event that touched the person deeply and left traces of the tension, fear, or some other strong emotion. When traces are left, it is logical that dreams with a corresponding theme arise more frequently.

There are similar varieties of dreams that are related to the clarity of an individual, that is, those related to the three existences and those related to the karmic traces of the individual. What is a dream of clarity? A dream of clarity manifests when there are secondary causes; through the secondary causes it manifests as clarity. We can even obtain advice and predictions for the future because there are secondary causes of future events. A dream of clarity generally manifests in the early morning. Why? Because when we first fall asleep, we sleep very deeply. Slowly we consume this heaviness and our sleep becomes lighter. As it becomes lighter, clarity can manifest more easily. If our practice of continuous presence succeeds, then karmic dreams diminish. This is because they are linked with tensions. The state of contemplation, or presence, represents total relaxation. Consequently, there will be no manifestation of tension. In the place of karmic dreams, you have more dreams of clarity.

Regarding the type of clarity dream related to the three existences, all human beings have in their nature infinite potential and unmanifest qualities. Although the sun shines constantly, sometimes we cannot see it due to cloud covering, while at other times, we can see between the clouds for a few moments. Similarly, sometimes the individual's clarity spontaneously appears. One result of this is the appearance of dreams of clarity.

People who are practicing Dharma try to relax. Through relaxing the body, energy, and mind, the elements and energies become balanced, and through this instant secondary cause different kinds of clarity dreams arise. This is particularly true for one who is doing practices related to the chakras[4] and the channels, which control the *prana* and energy.

For some individuals, these types of clarity dreams arise through the clarity of their minds even without their applying secondary methods to relax the body or control the energy. When a practitioner has matured or developed, there is a diminution of the obstacles that obscure the natural clarity of mind. Following the analogy of the sun, the clouds have now largely disappeared and the infinite rays of sunshine are able to manifest directly.

When all conditions are correct and the body, speech, and mind are relaxed due to a developed practice, then there appear many kinds of clarity dreams, some of which may anticipate a future event.

Also, like ordinary dreams that have karmic causes from past lives, clarity dreams of previous karma can reawaken. Depending on the dreamer's capacity, it might be possible to remember a past life in its entirety. One hundred or even one hundred thousand lives can be remembered in a dream. We can read about these extraordinary dreams appearing due to unobstructed clarity in accounts of the lives of bodhisattvas and arhats.

An example of the dreams of clarity that a practitioner might have as a result of the karmic traces accumulated during youth would be as follows. Earlier in life, a person may have met many extraordinary teachers, or received teachings and empowerments, or learned methods of practice. Later, that person can have dreams about these things in which he or she goes deeper into this knowledge. The person may even acquire within a dream knowledge or methods for practice that he or she has never heard before. One can have many interesting dreams of this type.

Clarity dreams related to recent experiences may arise as follows. A person reads something, perhaps a very important Dharma text or has a deep conversation about practicing Dharma. This may become the cause for dreams having to do with the past, the present, or even the future.

These are the types of clarity dreams. They are a continuation and development of the ordinary type of dream and arise primarily for practitioners who already have some experience working with their dreams or who have experience maintaining lucidity and awareness within the dream. They are the type of dreams that manifest through the clarity of one's state of mind, or *rigpa*.[5]

Many of the methods of practicing Dharma that are learned during waking can, upon development of dream awareness, be applied in the dream condition. In fact, one may develop these practices more easily and speedily within the Dream State if one has the capacity to dream lucidly. There are even some books that say that if a person applies a practice within a dream, the practice is nine times more effective than when it is applied during the waking hours.

The dream condition is unreal. When we discover this for ourselves within the dream, the immense power of this realization can eliminate obstacles related to conditioned vision. For this reason, dream practice is very important for liberating us from habits. We need this powerful assistance in particular because the emotional attachments, conditioning, and ego enhancement, which compose our normal life, have been strengthened over our many, many years. In a real sense, all the visions that we see in our lifetime are like the images of a dream. If we examine them well, the big dream of life and the smaller dreams of one night are not very different. If we truly see the essential nature of both, we will find that there really is no difference between them. If we can finally liberate ourselves from the chains of emotions, attachments, and ego by this realization, we have the possibility of ultimately becoming enlightened.

CHAPTER 2

The Practice of the Night

The night is very important for us because half our lives pass during it, but often we quietly sleep away all that time without any effort or commitment. There has to be real awareness that practice can occur at all times, even during sleep or eating. If this does not happen, progress on the path will be difficult. Therefore, the practice of the night is very important, and I will explain its theory and practice.

When someone says "practice of the night," we usually think of the practice of lucid dreaming. There are many explanations of lucid dreaming. But in the Dzogchen teaching, the practice of dreamwork, and the development of lucidity, is not fundamental. It is a secondary practice. In the case of dream practice, "secondary" means that this practice can arise spontaneously, or automatically, from doing the principal practice, which is called the "practice of natural light."

This practice, the practice of natural light, actually has to do with the state prior to dream. For example, a person falls asleep; "falls asleep" means that all of one's senses vanish into them, and thus they are sleeping. From that point on there is a passage, a period of transition, until dreams begin. That period may be long or it may be short.

For some people, the state of dreams begins almost immediately after falling asleep. But what does it mean that the state of dreams begins? It means that the mind begins to function again.

In contrast, that which is called the state of natural light is not a moment, or a state, in which the mind is functioning. It is the period beginning when you fall asleep and ending when the mind begins to function again. What exists after this? After this exists what we call the *milam bardo*.[1]

There is a correspondence between the states of sleep and dreams and our experiences when we die. When a person dies, first of all, the senses vanish. In speaking of bardos, we speak of the moment when the senses vanish into ourselves as the bardo of the moment of dying, or *chikhai bardo*. At this moment, the person has the many sensations of the disappearing, or withdrawing, of the senses.

After that comes a state like unconsciousness; it is similar to a faint. Then begins what is called the arising of four lights. Various tantras[2] explain this with some slight differences. Some divide it into four lights; some refer to five lights. The truth is that it is as if you had fainted and with the arising of lights, slowly, slowly consciousness is beginning to reawaken.

For example, the mind must begin working in order for reasoning to occur. First we must have an awareness of the senses. The mind begins to receive these perceptions, but there is no reasoning or thinking yet. Slowly, step by step, thinking arises.

There is the presence of the state of awareness and yet mind has not begun to enter into operations such as thinking. This is the passage through which one moves in what is called the state of natural light. It has always been considered that it is during this period that the practitioner of Tantra realizes themself. In Tantra, this period is also described as the moment in which one meets the mother light.[3] It is exactly in this moment after the faint, that awareness develops again, or reawakens.

In Tantric initiation, there are four sub-initiations, and the last of them is called the initiation of the word. If you have understood at that time, the master gives a kind of introduction to the nature of mind.[4] Even if you have not realized natural mind, but you have a lot of participation, commitment, and faith, and you practice with devotion, it is sometimes possible that in the moment of the last awakening of consciousness there will come a flash of recognition of natural mind, or *rigpa*. It is not easy, but if you have really had knowledge, it is possible. As you are passing, or moving through, there is the development of a series of lights, for which there are many explanations.

In the Dzogchen teaching, the last of these phases, the fifth light, is spoken of as *lhundrub*,[5] the state of self-perfectedness. In that moment you have a reawakening of consciousness. It is possible for you to recognize that which has been transmitted to you through direct introduction by the teacher. The experience of that transmission is what we call the experience of wisdom.

Let us use the analogy of the sun. Imagine that the sky is covered with clouds, and between these clouds you catch a glimpse of the sun. Even if the clouds have not allowed full sunlight, you have had an experience of what is meant by sun and sunlight. This experience is analogous to that of the experience of wisdom.

This knowledge is spoken of as the "son" knowledge, in contrast to the "mother" knowledge, or full experience. When we practice, we try to develop this son knowledge. This knowledge is the "son" of the "mother."

Some people succeed through practice in fully developing this knowledge and thus realize themselves totally in this life. It is said that such a person can realize the Body of Light.[6]

But even if you have not realized yourself totally, and yet have had experience of practice, then in the moment after death, in this state of lhundrub, when you encounter the mother light, you will recognize the full presence of wisdom before you return into the workings of the mind. The analogy that is used is that of a son uniting with his mother. The books speak of the meeting between the son light and the mother light, but what is really meant is that what we had only an example of, we now encounter in its fullness.

This state—as we proceed through the lights to the ultimate

light, the *lhundrub*, or light of self-perfectedness—is the state in which any and every practitioner of Tantrism realizes himself or herself. It is only after that experience that the state of *sidpai bardo* begins. Up to that point, we experience the *chönyid bardo*, the bardo of the *dharmata*. Why do we call it the *dharmata*? Because it represents our actual underlying state, or underlying consciousness.

The *sidpai bardo* begins after the *chönyid bardo*. This is the bardo as one normally knows it, the bardo of existence. In other words, it is where the workings of the mind begin again. It is as if we had now gone into the state of dream. As in dream you can dream anything, and then at a certain moment, you wake up and another day begins, so it is considered that you come out of the bardo and another existence begins. This existence is determined by its karmic vision, and that is how you transmigrate. This is how we continue day in, night out.

So, we see that the state of the bardos is not something to be read about or understood abstractly. It is relevant to practice. The way to practice for death and the *sidpai bardo* is to do this practice of natural light. If you have become knowledgeable of, or have awareness of, the state of natural light, you will also have that awareness and presence in the moment of dying. If you are capable of dying with presence and awareness, it means you are knowledgeable about the manifestations of light. In this case, you will have no difficulty recognizing the mother light.

To repeat: with the beginning of the bardo of existence, the functioning or working of the mind, what is called the mental body, also begins. This is equivalent to the arising of the state of dreams. In the practice we do, there has to be an awareness of, or mastery of, the state of natural light. When one has an awareness of the presence of this state of natural light, then even if afterward the state of dreams arises, one spontaneously becomes lucidly aware that one is dreaming while dreaming, and automatically one achieves mastery of one's dreams. This means that the dream does not condition the person, but the person governs his or her dream. For this reason, the practice of dreams is secondary. I cannot overemphasize how extremely important it is to do the practice of natural light.

When we start to dream, as previously mentioned, we may have one of two general types of dreams. One type is karmic dreams and the other is dreams of clarity. In addition to those dreams reflecting karma from our current life, karmic dreams can also be linked to our past lives.

The other type of dreams are dreams of clarity. Why do we have dreams of clarity? Because everybody, since the beginning, has infinite potentiality; that is a quality of the natural mind that we all possess. Sometimes, even if we are not doing a particular practice, a dream of clarity will manifest because we have that nature. If you are doing the practice of the night and becoming more familiar with it, then not only occasionally but on a regular basis you will become familiar with manifestations of dreams of clarity.

You may now understand what the theory is and its importance. Now I will explain how you practice it.

If you are an agitated person, then before you go to sleep, you can do a little deep breathing to regulate the flow of air and calm yourself. Then concentrate on a white Tibetan syllable ༀ at the center of your body. If you prefer an English *A*, it is acceptable. The important thing is that it corresponds in your mind to the sound *ahh*. It is important that when you see that letter, you automatically know what its sound is.

If you do not succeed in concentrating and seeing this ༀ at first, it may be that you do not know how to visualize. Try writing an ༀ on a piece of paper, put it in front of you and stare at it for a while. Close your eyes and this ༀ will appear before your mind immediately. In this way you will get a more precise image.

So, you try to concentrate on this white ༀ. Or you fix on the presence of this white ༀ and you stay with it as long as you can.

You can also do a kind of training to have greater precision in feeling this presence: imagine that from the central ཨ, which is viewed at heart level within your body, a second arises, and from the second, a third arises, until you can see a chain of ཨs going up to the crown of the head. Then you visualize these ཨs coming back down. You can repeat this a number of times if you do not fall asleep immediately. Whenever you have difficulty in feeling the presence of the ཨ it is very useful and important to do this chain. This is a way of charging your clarity.

The most important point is that when you fall asleep, you try to have this ཨ present. Initially, it should be accurate and sharp; afterward, you relax. Relaxing does not mean you drop the ཨ or that you give it up. You retain a sense of its presence, and you relax, and thus you fall asleep.

You should try to do the practice of natural light each night, just as you should try to be in the state of contemplation continually. For every moment and every activity there are ways to do Dzogchen practice. If, however, Dzogchen practice of the night is difficult for you, and you have had more experience doing Tantric-style dream practice, and you have had an initiation on a particular deity, then perhaps it would be useful for you to continue with your Tantric practice. For example, if you do the practice of Vajrayogini,[7] then upon sleeping, you should try to visualize a very tiny Vajrayogini at the center of your body. We call this tiny being Jnanasattva, which means "wisdom manifestation."

You keep this presence and continue your sleep. There are other visualization practices similar to Guruyoga[8] in Tantric dream practices. For example, you might visualize Vajradhara[9] as the unification of all your gurus and manifest that visualization in the center of your body. You would keep the presence of this visualization, relax, and slowly, slowly go to sleep. Because these are Tantric exercises, you should practice only the special instructions you receive from your master.

By contrast, in Dzogchen we generally do the visualization of the white ཨ, as described above, for the purpose of coordinating the energy. We visualize the white ཨ at the center of the body. After having manifested this white, luminous ཨ, we slowly relax. We relax slowly but completely when we do this visualization so as not to have tension. If we do not relax completely, we will be unable to sleep. We must spontaneously manifest the white ཨ without thinking, without creating, and then relax all effort and go to sleep.

In order to remind yourself to visualize this white ཨ and to do the Dzogchen practice of the night, it is very useful to put a picture or a sign of a white ཨ near your bed. No one will know what it is; perhaps they will think it is a piece of artwork. You, however, will know its precise function.

It is also very important to remember the practice of the white ཨ when you awaken in the morning. If possible, you may sound *ahh* immediately. If you cannot sound loudly because there is someone else sleeping, it is enough that you exhale with *ahh*. As long as you can hear yourself and feel the presence of that white ཨ, this is a method of Guruyoga. It is not necessary to say many words or prayers; simply having the presence of the white ཨ and recognizing that the ཨ is the unification of the mind of all your gurus is sufficient. Then you integrate this into a state of contemplation, or *rigpa*.

Starting your morning yoga in this way is wonderful and will help you very much with all your practices and particularly your practice of the night. There is a kind of a connection that you make by remembering the white ཨ when you are going to sleep and, then again, in the morning.

For those who have not practiced this before, the first, second, or third time you attempt it you may not succeed at all. In fact, you may find you try it a little and then suddenly you are asleep. Like anything, until you have learned it, it is difficult, but if you exert your will power, it will become familiar to you.

If you are capable of falling asleep like this, you will find the full presence of the state of natural light. When you fall asleep, you are asleep with virtually full awareness. If you have this presence of mind when entering into the state of dreams, it is easy to recognize that you are dreaming. It may not happen right away; you may arrive slowly at this result.

Even if this natural light does not occur immediately, the first results will begin to show themselves in the state of dreams. You may find yourself dreaming strange dreams. What do I mean by strange dreams? As mentioned above, we normally have two types of dreams. The karmic type comes from the traces of our difficulties, problems, memories, and preoccupation. Then there is the type of dream in which our natural clarity manifests. For example, toward morning, interesting dreams of things you have never thought about may occur, things that have no relationship to the traces of your thought and past but are more linked to your clarity. If you have practiced the natural light, dreams of natural clarity will manifest more frequently.

If you persevere in this practice of recognizing the state of natural light, it will progressively become easier to repeat the lucid recognition that you are dreaming. There will arise a steady awareness within the dream, and you will know that you are dreaming. When you look in a mirror, you see a reflection. Regardless of whether it is beautiful or ugly, you know that it is a reflection. This is similar to knowing that a dream is a dream, to being lucid. Whether the dream is tragic or ecstatic, you are aware that it is merely a dream.

Awareness within the Dream State becomes a way to develop oneself and to break one's heavy conditioning. With this awareness, one can manipulate the dream material. For example, one can dream whatever one wishes, or one can pick up a desired theme. One can continue dreaming from where one left off on a previous occasion.

Within the Tantric system, the specific dream yoga practice is oriented toward preparing the practitioner for the bardo after the time of death. This is not the case in the Dzogchen system. In the Dzogchen system, it is not necessary that one commit oneself to working on dreams. That will arise naturally out of the practice of natural light. The most important thing for this practice, as I have described, is to do the particular visualization of the white ཨ before sleeping. In doing this visualization, we use the working of the mind in order to eventually go beyond the mind.

The position you are in while practicing this visualization is not ultimately important. Many people do this visualization practice after they are lying in bed. You must see what kind of person you are. One person may fall asleep merely by shutting his or her eyes, while another person might need to take a sleeping pill.

Let us take the example of the person who lies down and immediately falls asleep. If this person becomes distracted from his or her practice for a moment, he or she is already asleep. This is the type of person for whom a particular physical position might be useful. If the practitioner is a male, it may be beneficial for him to lie on his right side. Assuming he does not have a cold that has blocked his breathing, it might also be useful for him to close the right nostril with his hand.

For women, the position is reversed. A woman should lie on her left side and try to block her left nostril. I am not saying to stop breathing if you have a cold. This of course would not be a good thing. But what usually happens is that when you lie down on your side and the unclosed nostril is congested, within a few minutes that nostril will open.

The reason that the positions are reversed for men and women has to do with the solar and lunar channels.[10] We take these positions to make it easier to enter the state of contemplation, or presence of the natural light. If they make your sleep more difficult, then they are not recommended. That is why these positions are primarily for a person who tends to fall asleep easily.

Let us consider for a moment the opposite situation, that of a person who has real problems falling asleep. In such a case, it would not be advisable to do this kind of visualization practice or to take this position. It is likely that this type of person would merely become more nervous and perhaps not sleep at all. An alternative for people of this type would be for them to observe their thoughts. Whatever thoughts arise should be merely observed. Then, in this state of observing the thoughts without becoming involved or conditioned by them, one sleeps. As long as one is not distracted, this is something that anyone can do without creating obstacles to falling asleep.

If you have difficulty sleeping at night, there are other practices you may employ to assist you. For example, this difficulty often means that you need to coordinate the energy and function of the different elements within your body. If your energy is disordered, it prevents you from sleeping. In this case, a deep breathing practice done repeatedly can be beneficial. You might do the ninefold purification breathing[11] before going to sleep. There are also physical exercises such as a series of eight movements[12] found in Yantra Yoga that can help develop your capacity for correct breathing and also balance your energies as an aid to sleeping.

In addition, there are Tibetan medicines to assist a person who has difficulty sleeping. Unlike sleeping pills, they do not cause dependence or other side effects. These medicines, such as Agar 35 and Vimala[13] can be used for one or two months—as long as you need, really—and will not cause any negative side effects. Rather, they will help your health and coordinate your energy. When you do not need the medicine anymore, you can stop without withdrawal symptoms or negative effects. That is the benefit of these Tibetan medicines.

If you have become habituated to Western sleeping pills, you can initially alternate them with Tibetan pills in order to lessen the dependency. One night you use Western medicine, and the next night you use Agar 35. After one or two weeks of alternating, you will be able to stop taking the Western medicine without a problem.

You must not think only of Tibetan medicine when it comes to assuring a good night's sleep. You should also work with breathing in the manner previously mentioned, as this is very related to sleep.

Sometimes you cannot sleep because one of your three humors[14] is disturbed. When the wind humor is disturbed, one has particular trouble sleeping. Wind is linked with *prana*, or energy. When *prana* is disturbed, it is difficult to sleep. For more information on this you can consult books on Tibetan medicine. In a book I wrote[15] on the topic, there is an explanation of the three humors and how to overcome problems. For example, to overcome problems related to wind disease, it is helpful to go to bed earlier in the evening, to sleep with warm clothes, and to have something like soup to eat just before going to bed. If you are not sleeping at night, and instead of relaxing, you work hard until late hours, or you eat raw vegetables, this may further aggravate the condition. There are many things to learn in Tibetan medical books.

Everything is related. First try these preparations so you can fall asleep. If you have succeeded, then you can do the practice of the night. If your situation is somewhere between falling asleep immediately and not being able to fall asleep, then visualize a white ཨ, or *A*, but one that is not very bright. If you have a problem falling asleep, you must not visualize the white ཨ as too bright. You could also visualize it in a sphere of five colors. This makes it easier to fall asleep. There are many kinds of people and many situations; we should know about all of them.

If you do this practice with commitment, slowly you may become a master of your dreams. As you have more awareness and more dreams of clarity, dreaming becomes a practice. If you are aware in the dream, you can experience many things within the Dream State. It is easier to develop your practices in a dream than in the daytime. In the daytime we are limited by our material body, but in a dream the functioning of our mind and our consciousness of the senses are unhindered. We can have more clarity. Thus, there are more possibilities. For example, it is possible to practice advanced Dzogchen practices of *thödgal*[16] and the Dzogchen *Longde*.[17] If you practice these in the daytime, you can certainly have meditative experiences, but in a dream you can have experiences beyond the limitations of the material body. That is why the practice is very important. In the daytime, all the experiences we have are very much conditioned by our attachment and tension. We feel that everything is concrete. In a dream, we may initially feel that everything is concrete but then suddenly remember that it is a dream. When you are aware in a dream, you know you are dreaming and that it is unreal. You know you are in a state of unreality. Once you have this experience, you can also make discoveries about your daily life, for example, something about your major attachments. The ultimate result is to diminish your tension.

As I mentioned, if one has achieved sufficient mastery of dreams, one can transform them. If I am dreaming of something ugly, I could transform it into something beautiful, I could cause the dream to deal with some theme or argument that I have chosen, or I could play out some fantasy of my imagination. I could visit a paradise or contact a certain teacher. There are many things one can do; one can oftentimes work out the dream as one wishes. This can become a test of one's actual progress.

For those people who find it difficult to have the kind of presence I've described, the practice of the dark retreat[18] is very useful. After two days or three days in the dark, you lose your sense of day and night. Your sleep becomes lighter and lighter. You sleep and wake up, sleep and wake up. Such a retreat offers a good opportunity to develop your presence and clarity. In this environment you can more easily discover what it means to have presence when you are sleeping. Your waking and sleeping states thus become integrated.

Normally, for a practitioner, one of the principal ways that signs of progress manifest is through dreams. Sometimes there occurs, in dream, an intervention on behalf of the practitioner. For example, if I am doing something wrong, I may have a communication through a dream. This may come by way of a transmission of the teaching. It may also come through the protectors of the teaching or the dakinis.

Many problems can be resolved through the transmission that comes in dream. You can't expect that you are going to have the master at your beck and call in the flesh all your life.

When I, for example, had been in Italy for about three years, I had a dream of my master Changchub Dorje.[19] In the dream I actually felt that I had returned to Tibet. It seemed so real, and I was in fact a bit frightened about the Chinese. I was worried, and I said to myself, "Who knows if the Chinese will let me out again." Then I met my teacher. I felt embarrassed, as my intention was to greet him quickly and then get out of there and go back to Italy. My master said to me, "It has been many years that we haven't seen each other. How is your practice going?" I said, "Well, like this and like that." And he asked, "What practice have you been doing?" I explained that I had been doing my best to take into daily life the practice of tregchöd.[20] "You haven't been doing any of the practice of thödgal?" he continued. And I said, "Well, no, I haven't been doing the thödgal." He asked, "Well, why not?" "Well," I answered, "because you told me that I had to perfect the tregchöd first. I had to get it very stable. So I'm working to perfect and make very stable my tregchöd." He said, "Well, do you have any doubts about your knowledge of thödgal?" I said, "No, no, I don't have any doubts. I just haven't been doing that practice." He said, "Well you better get to it. Do the practice of thödgal. That is very important." I said, "Okay, that's what I'll be doing from now on." He said, "Now listen, if you do have any doubts about thödgal, or anything you don't understand clearly, go ask Jigmed Lingpa."[21] I said, "Where is Jigmed Lingpa?" "Up the mountain there, in the cave," he answered. "Up where?" I asked, because right behind the village where my master is, there is a sheer cliff. When I was living with my master, I went up that mountain many times to collect medicines. I know perfectly well there is no cave up there. At least in those times there was no cave. I thought to myself, "Well, why is he telling me there's a cave up there?" The master became wrathful. He said, "If you really want to understand something, you'll get up there and find Jigmed Lingpa in that cave."

So I didn't argue anymore. I was very curious about it. I went out and started climbing up the mountain to see where the cave was. A certain part of the rock face is white, but in this dream I found it a little bit different from how it had been. It was all carved with innumerable letters, which I could read in Tibetan. It seemed like a tantra. I thought, "This is very strange. It wasn't like that before." And I thought to myself, "Well, from walking and climbing over this tantra, I'm going to accumulate some bad actions." This is a Tibetan way of thinking about things. So with this preoccupation, I started reciting the one-hundred-syllable mantra.[22] Then slowly, slowly I continued to climb up.

At a certain point there was a sort of curved rock that I had to climb on; this rock appeared to be a title page, with the title of the tantra that I'd just been climbing over. It was called the *Trödral tönsal nyingpoi gyud*. *Trödral* means "beyond concept"; *tönsal* means "to clarify the meaning"; *nyingpoi* means "the essence." Later I discovered that there actually is a tantra of that name.

So then I climbed up and slowly, slowly approached the very peak of the mountain, and there was a cave. Coming close, I looked inside this rather large cave. At the very center, there was a stone—a white boulder, hard and like granite. It was not a tiny stone; it was a big boulder. Sitting on this rock was a little boy. I'm sure that he wasn't more than seven or eight years old. I looked around. There was nobody else in there. I said to myself, "This is pretty strange. Jigmed Lingpa lived a long time ago. He couldn't be a little boy like that." Meanwhile this little boy was looking at me. I thought to myself, "Well, since my master told me to come up here and meet Jigmed Lingpa, who knows, maybe this is some kind of emanation of Jigmed Lingpa." I thought that I had better behave well toward him.

So I directly approached the child. He was wearing a garment that was like a transparent blue shirt. He had nothing else on. He had long hair, but not tied up like that of a yogi. He just looked like a normal little boy. I found this pretty strange. So I came up right in front of him. I said, "Master Changchub Dorje sent me to you." The little boy looked at me. He looked almost as if he were surprised to hear this. Looking at the boy I began to doubt him, but I watched what he was doing. Finally he gestured me to sit down. When I sat down, he reached and touched the back of his head, and brought forth a roll of paper, a scroll. He opened the scroll and began to read from it. When he read, it was in the voice of a little boy, but he was not giving a teaching or an explanation. He was reading. He read four or five sentences. Immediately upon hearing his voice, I realized that the scroll was a tantra. At that moment it struck me, "Oh it's true, it is Jigmed Lingpa," because it could hardly be some ordinary little boy who can produce a scroll and then read in this fashion. And with this emotion, this startling thought, I awoke from the dream. Afterward I did elaborate research to find those texts, and I found specific texts on the Dzogchen *thödgal* practice. This is an example of the fact that a relationship between master and disciple always exists regardless of questions of time and distance. My master was far, far away in Tibet; I was living in Europe.

These are some of the possibilities that can occur within dreams as one's practice progresses.

If you fall asleep with the presence of the ༀ, you may find yourself waking in the morning with it still present. You can then assume that you have spent the entire night in practice. As the night is rather long, and you have nothing else to do but sleep, it is very important to utilize the time. Night can become, for a practitioner, even more important than the practice of the day.

The final goal of dream practice is to make dreams become awareness and, there, at that ultimate point, dreams actually cease. You use your practice so that your dreams influence daily life. This is the principal practice of the nighttime. You should try to do the practice of natural light each night, just as you should try to be in the state of contemplation continually. For every morning and every activity there are ways to do Dzogchen practice.

CHAPTER 3

The Methods of Practicing
the Essence of Dreams[1]

The five subdivisions to cut attachment to dreams are: the explanations of how to practice the essence of channels and *prana*, dreams, illusory body, clear light, and transference. Four of these subdivisions, with the exception of practicing the essence of channels and *prana*, are covered in this book.

The first subdivision, not included, explains how to practice the essence of channels and *prana*. This includes learning *kumbhaka*[2] breathing from a qualified Yantra Yoga teacher and receiving Dzogchen transmission from a qualified master. It is very beneficial for a practitioner who desires success in dreamwork also to learn how to control *prana*.

The second subdivision is addressed in this chapter. This section is the explanation of how to practice the Essence of Dreams.

As previously mentioned, let us review preparations for dreamwork as well as the actual practice. Regarding preparation, it may be helpful for one to conduct a retreat to first practice concentrating on the six syllables and their purification.[3] After doing this practice for some time, many disordered dreams may appear. The arising of numerous disordered dreams is a sign that preparation is complete and that one can proceed to the practice.

The explanation of how to practice the Essence of Dreams has two subdivisions. These are, first, the explanation of the methods to apply the key points of dreams and, second, the explanation of the key points about performing actions within dreams.

Regarding the methods of application, there are three essential subdivisions. The first is to examine the dream, the second to control it, and the third to distinguish and recognize the *pagchag*, or karmic traces. As preparation for examining the dream, it is advisable to relax the body, through baths and massage for example, each night before sleeping. One must then resolve with full intention to progress on the path toward full awareness and lucidity within dreams and never be distracted from the one-pointed intention, "I will be aware of dreams."

One may initially make use of the positions previously mentioned to facilitate the practice. A practitioner thus lies down on his or her side—the right side having to do with clarity, the left with void for men (and the reverse for women)—and closes the corresponding nostril with a finger of the corresponding hand, which lies under one's cheek. As the left side governs, or allows, the void to operate, and the right side helps with the operation of clarity, it may be preferable, initially, for men to lie on the left side, thus promoting clarity—the work of the unimpeded right, and vice versa for women. Later as one's practice becomes stable, position will not be important.

If there is no clarity, as if one has not had any dreams, that means there is a problem that sleep is too deep. In this case, one should elevate the bed or pillow, or sleep with a light on, or with the window open. One may also experiment using lighter or fewer covers, letting more air into the sleeping place, or moving to a more open spot. If dreams still do not come regularly, one may also experiment by sleeping in whichever way one finds comfortable, on either the right or the left side.

If the dreams are still not clear, visualize a glowing white *thigle* at the location of the third eye in your forehead. If there is still nothing, visualize this white bead with increasing radiance each successive night. Gradually, by concentrating the mind in this fashion, whatever dreams arise will be clear. If, due to the aforementioned concentration, it is difficult to fall asleep, then alternatively visualize a red letter ཨ at the throat. If this is difficult, a red bead will suffice. If you still do not remember dreams, visualize the red letter or bead as increasingly more luminous each successive night.

If difficulty persists, think of a white bead on your forehead. These concentrations are performed only if dreams are not remembered.

If you are able to fall asleep in this state of concentration, the dreams that arise will definitely be clear. Your dreams will also become more associated with clarity, and slowly, slowly you will develop greater awareness.

Having examined dreams in this way, one may now train to control them. If one's dreams are clear, but one is not lucid within the Dream State, then with great determination train the mind by thinking "all daytime visions are a dream." Continually remind yourself that all that you see and all that is done is none other than a dream. By seeing everything throughout the day as if it were a dream, dream and awareness are thoroughly mixed. If you concentrate a great deal during the day, imagining that you are living a dream, then during the night the dream itself will also seem less real. The subject, that which experiences the dream, is the mind. By holding the thought that all is a dream, you begin to dissolve this "subject." That is, the mind begins to dissolve itself, automatically.

Or, to put it another way, when the object, or vision, is dissolved, the action turns back toward the subject, causing complete dissolution. Thus, neither vision nor dream exists any longer. One finds that the subject is not concrete and that vision is only a "reflection." One thus becomes aware of the true nature of both. Vision created by karma and the psychic "tail," or background imprint, is the origin of all illusions. If authentic awareness of the illusory reality arises, one arrives at the disappearance of "solid reality." Realization means true understanding of the waking state and the Dream State.

Subsequently, before sleeping, continue to focus well on the red ᢀ in the throat. Focusing in this way before falling asleep unites the *lung*, or *prana*, there with concentration. Then after falling asleep without having been kept awake and distracted by the visualization of the radiant red letter ᢀ in the throat, dreams will be recognized as dreams. Regarding this process, at first when nightmares arise with frightening subjects such as floods, fires, vicious dogs (or other animals), enemies, precipices, etc., then due to shock you may instantly become lucid and think, "This is a dream." This is named "recognizing a harsh dream," or "distinguishing the dream by violent means." Achieving lucidity in this manner is relatively common; once one has had that recognition and is familiar with lucidity, one may recognize all dreams, whether the content is good or bad.

After one can recognize dreams while dreaming, one earnestly trains with daytime mental objects to magically manifest many different visions. For example, manifesting all kinds of peaceful, joyous, and wrathful divine figures, as well as varieties of sentient beings through fantasy. Just as one trains with these mental objects in the daytime, one becomes able to manifest them clearly in dreams at night.

Further, one continues to train with daytime mental objects. Practice by transforming deities into *nagas* (snake-like beings), *nagas* into deities, males into females, females into males, big things into little things, little things into big things, white color into red color, red color into white color, one into many, and many into one, etc. Subsequently, one is also able to manifest these daytime objects clearly in dreams at night.

Intense concentration on a theme or on any subject will lead to its arising within a dream. If you wish to cause yourself to dream of a Tibetan deity, for example, think of transforming yourself into that deity by concentrating intensely on the deity. Continued progress in dreamwork, even after lucid awareness is commonly achieved, depends very much on the activities of the day.

Knowing the true nature of the dream, you may subsequently transform it. If you dream of a snake, for example, upon recognizing that you are dreaming, you should transform the snake into whatever you like, perhaps a man. Thus, it is not the dream that commands the dreamer but the dreamer who commands the dream. When you have become able to change the dream, develop your skill by further scrambling the dream elements, for example, putting what is in the east in the west, multiplying or condensing the elements, turning things upside down, putting high things low, or making what is big, small. This process applies not only to forms but also to sensations. If you dream of something pleasing, transform it into something unpleasant. Systematically reverse everything. Amid intentional transformation, spontaneous images may arise. For example, if you dream that you are in a forest and choose to change the situation and place yourself in a desert, some items that appear may be different from what you intended to project. As one progresses and manages to maintain meditative awareness, experiences of clarity arise spontaneously.

After that, one continues to train by fantasizing traveling to all kinds of places that one has never before visited—including the pure realms. With this training, one becomes able to travel to these places in dreams at night. One also trains by imagining meeting people regardless of whether or not one knows them or knew them in the past and engaging them in all manner of conversations about subjects in which one is interested. Then one may travel to all kinds of pure realms, meet with many masters and *rigdzins*, whether or not one has met them previously, and obtain all kinds of profound teachings and instructions from them. By earnestly training with great diligence in this way, one quickly becomes proficient in dream practice.

The third method for applying the key points of dreams pertains to the method to recognize karmic traces of dreams. If, during the night, one dreams predominantly about places and homes to which one was attached, this is because these dreams are largely due to karmic traces of previous attachments. If there arise too many images of the past, of childhood, for example, or even of other lives, one could say that the dreams are influenced by the psychic "tail," or background of these images. In this case, transformation of the dream may become a little difficult. If, on the other hand, karmic traces of previous dreams are small, it will be very easy to transform one's dreams.

If one's dreams at night are largely about current circumstances, then, because one can analyze the karmic traces of the dream, it is very easy to transform the dream. In this case, it is possible to train and become proficient even within three or four days.

If one's dreams about travel to unknown places or meetings with unfamiliar people predominate, it may be quite hard to put an end to dreaming or to exhaust the Dream State. These types of dreams render it difficult to cut through dreams. Also, if one dreams of a confused mixture of the three aforementioned aspects, that is due to some attachment to one's previous mental objects being mixed with some current circumstances and some unfamiliar beings. This is called the "union of the three karmic traces (*pagchag sumdu*)." In this situation it is also very difficult to decisively cut through dreams. It is an indication that the process of transcending the Dream State will be long and extremely difficult. If we have obstacles that hinder our final overcoming of dreams, we must make a deeper commitment.

The second subdivision of how to practice the Essence of Dreams explains the key points about performing actions within dreams. It has eight subdivisions. These are the methods to train, transform, dissolve, disorder, stabilize, essentialize, hold, and reverse dreams.

Training

In the daytime, understanding the nature of dreams, transform whatever manifestations one has dreamed during the previous night into various mental objects. Train the mind that all external manifestations are not real and look directly into the essential nature of who is doing this training. It is very important to leave whatever manifests in its naked essence, beyond any source or foundation.

Recognize that whatever manifests is one's self-manifestation, with no reference point, no existence, no foundation, and no identity. Training in a one-pointed way, one becomes familiar with this practice, and whatever phenomena appear concretely are only illusions, dreams arising in oneself, delusive visions of karma and karmic traces, arid delusive attachments—all of which dissolve in their own nature.

Also, while dreaming at night, one will not be distracted from this state. So, day and night one is never separate from the chakra of the real condition.

Transforming

For the second action, the method of transforming dreams, there are two subdivisions. The first is the essential point to transform dreams into manifestations. For this purpose, during the daytime, utilize a mirror as a support. Train by transforming one reflection into another. For example, transform all manifestations into divine figures, etc. This exercise will assist you in transforming dreams during the nighttime, and gradually your capacity to transform will become more elaborate. For example, by beginning to reconfigure dream objects into animals within the Dream State, one will discover the capacity to transform whatever manifests into mandalas of deities, the pure realms, the eight examples of illusions, etc.

Next are the key points for transforming dreams into emptiness. As one continues toward mastery of the Dream State, the next principal technique is the mixing of daytime vision and dreams. One must constantly carry one's awareness into one's dreams.

As soon as the dream arises, instantly be aware that it is unreal. One must also bring this same recognition of unreality to one's daily vision.

As we develop our awareness of the dream nature, we may use dreams to deepen our meditative awareness. For example, a meditator who penetrates to the nature of "vision" (of phenomenal existence) finds it void. This perception of the emptiness of vision can then be transferred to the dream. If, while dreaming, you are not only aware that you are dreaming but also conscious that all vision is an illusion, you penetrate to the Void at its heart. Thus, a dream can be transformed into the knowledge of emptiness, *shunyata*.

As one steadily meditates that the delusive manifestations of daytime existence instantly become empty, like clouds vanishing into the sky or smoke disappearing into space, it carries over into the Dream State. Within your dreams, you will be able to manifest emptiness beyond thought. Continue training the mind with this awareness practice to realize that no external manifestations are real. Leave whatever manifests in its naked essence, beyond source, reference point, or foundation.

Dissolving

The next subdivision of action is the method for dissolving dreams. In the daytime, one does not consider the dream manifestations to be real and when actually dreaming, one is lucid. Although awareness of the true nature of the dream may enhance one's meditative awareness, there is also the danger that, by becoming skilled at the transformation of dream images, one may become attached. This attachment must be overcome. Without pride in the ability to train and transform, one cuts attachment through recognizing the nonreality and insubstantiality of all that arises.

The principal means of cutting attachment through the dream experiences are three. First, during the day, do not dwell upon the dreams you have had. Second, while actually dreaming, watch without judging, without pleasure or fear, regardless of whether the visions seem positive or negative and thus might provoke joy or unhappiness—that is, attachment. Third, while dreaming, and then afterward, do not "clarify" what is "subject" from what is "object"—that is, do not consider which of the images that appear are real. By proceeding in these ways, you will find that complex dreams gradually simplify, lighten, and eventually may vanish completely. Thus, all that was conditioned will be liberated. At this point, dreaming ends. On the outside, one's presence does not become attached to manifestation. On the inside also, one's instant presence is not attached to the reflections that manifest directly. Without being conditioned by the concept of connecting the duality of manifestation and mind, totally beyond all subject and object, one relaxes in the spacious radiant depth of self-luminous *rigpa*, without mental fabrication of anything.

Progressing with the practice, at first there are coarse dreams, then subtle dreams, then traces of dreams forgotten, then more and more subtle dreams, and finally no dreams. At the time without dreams, even while sleeping, vivid appearances like daytime visions manifest to the individual senses. By integrating sleep with the clear light, one abides in the dimension beyond attachment to any appearance.

Disordering

For the explanation of the method to disorder dreams, "disordering dreams" means working with the energy of dreams. Transform the manifestations of the east, at a particular moment, into the west, and transform the manifestations of the west into the east. Similarly, by training to disorder into an undefined state all the various categories of things that can be perceived—like disordering joy into sorrow, nonconceptual into conceptual, conceptual into non-conceptual, etc.—it becomes easy to be proficient in disordering dreams. By also disordering into an undefined state the configuration of *prana* and mind in the locations of the four or five chakras, one quickly becomes proficient in disordering dreams.

Stabilizing

The key points to explain the method of stabilizing dreams are as follows. To stabilize means "to fully establish." The channels are stabilized when the body is in the sleeping position of the lion in accordance with whether one is male or female. Mind is stabilized by visualizing a radiant red ཨ in the throat. Dreams are stabilized when one falls asleep without being distracted by other thoughts. Then, although asleep, without falling under the power of dualistic considerations—like some manifested aspect of experience or some consciousness aspect of experience—one looks nakedly at the very essence of the experience without being bound by the chains of attachment. One establishes stabilization in that exact moment of direct seeing that recognizes the precise state of naked liberation.

Essentializing

The special technique to manifest lucid dreams is, at bedtime, to visualize the letter ཨ in the center of the throat and fall asleep in that dimension while controlling the channels.

At that time, all manifestations are integrated with the state of understanding. One undistractedly practices "liberation while arising" with all manifestations of dreams and daytime experience that occur impartially in an endless series.

Holding

The following action, the method to hold dreams, is a very precious oral instruction for all dreams. In order to enter the *thigle* network of *prana*, one slowly exhales the breathe while in the sleeping position of the lion. Then one imagines that while inhaling through the nose, the entire universe—samsara and nirvana—dissolves back through the nose and into the heart chakra, and the *prana* is held inside. Then, visualizing the Tibetan syllable HAM in the head and *thigles* descending from it, all manifestations freely melt in bliss.

One visualizes the primordial state of *rigpa* as a bright and shining radiant, white ᰉ within a *thigle* of five colors, like beautiful reflections in the mirror of one's heart. One meditates by holding the mind one-pointedly for a long time in that total state where one practices with the unreality of dreams that liberate while arising.

Reversing

Lastly, there is the method to reverse dreams. Fixing the mind on a clear red ᰉ in a tent-like dimension within the middle of the throat chakra, one falls asleep holding *prana* and luminous energy in the throat. In this manner, all manifestations are reversed upward from the heart chakra into the throat chakra. At this moment, without focusing on anything, one enters the primordial dimension, the naturally pristine condition of the expansive space. Abiding in the primordial purity of emptiness, all manifestations go beyond concepts into the real condition, and all daytime appearances, dreams, views, and meditations are left freely.

When this is experienced, even though the practitioner's frame of reference may not be perfect, persons with superior capacity are able to stop the continuity of the dream. Persons with medium diligence are able to quickly dissolve the dream, and those of lower diligence, after changing all dreams into good karmic tendencies, finally also become able to stop the continuity of the dream.

These practitioners at first dream many dreams, some of which have a very clear quality. Gradually, with practice, dreams decrease and, from the beginning, those of superior diligence have dreams whose quality is increasingly subtle and faint. Those of medium diligence have very clear dreams from the beginning, while those of lower diligence initially have very unclear dreams that gradually lighten.

In progression, one at first develops the capacity to become lucid within the dream. In the middle stage, one develops the capacity to change dreams into dreams with positive karmic tendencies. In the later stage, the practitioner ceases dreaming, as sleep becomes indistinguishable from the clear light and all dreams dissolve into it. This stage is called "dreams dissolve into the clear light."

CHAPTER 4

The Illusory Body

The following is the explanation of the third subdivision of meditation practices to cut attachment to dreams: The Method to Practice the Essence of Illusory Body.[1]

To develop the illusory body, it is necessary to have experience based upon dream practice. To proceed during the daytime, because appearances and all outer and inner phenomena, which arise like diverse reflections in a mirror, are nothing more than radiant manifestations of emptiness that have no intrinsic self-nature, there is nothing one should consider to really exist. By means of an undistracted intention, which considers that all inanimate and animate phenomena are manifestations of illusions and reflections, one meditates that whatever manifests is an illusion or reflection.

In particular, each reflection arising "as within the mirror," whether putting on clothes, wearing jewelry, making praises, or speaking unpleasant things, etc., is only the form of this or that arising within the mirror and cannot produce any benefit or harm. Ultimately, one is able to experience with certainty that nothing exists in truth. Similarly, one understands that self and other, enemy and friend, food and clothes, pleasant and unpleasant, joy and sorrow, attachment and aversion—whatever phenomenon of samsara or nirvana arises, whatever is perceived, whatever manifests—in the very moment of their manifestation have no essence, like a reflection in a mirror. Because of this, the nonreality of delusive manifestations and the nature of illusion become perfected in one's life-stream. One's own body is thus experienced as an illusory body and, without difficulty, one recognizes the illusory body of the bardo.

During the nighttime, understanding that all manifestations are dreams, because one diligently practices to realize that all inanimate and animate phenomena of the universe have the nature of illusions or dreams, all delusive manifestations of birth and death, denial and affirmation are recognized to be dreams and illusions. That is, when one is able to manifest like this inside a dream, one becomes free of attachment to any phenomenon that manifests anywhere.

Practicing like this day and night, one is not attached to delusive manifestations as reality, one's body manifests like a kind of immaterial shadow, and one is able to see its nonexistence. One's body does not cast a shadow, one is able to recognize the illusory body of the bardo, and one's rebirth in the future will be exalted.

CHAPTER 5

The Essential Practice of Clear Light

Editor's note: When a particular practice has a designated time, such as "dusk" or "midnight," it is important to understand that this is relative to one's own cycle of sleep rather than the actual time of day. For example, when one is told that a practice is to be done at dusk, this should be taken to mean that it is to be done any time before sleeping; its practice is not restricted solely to the evening hours.

The methods to practice clear light are related to the four time divisions of day, evening, midnight, and dawn.

The explanation of daytime practice includes methods for contemplation and post-contemplation. Here is the method to practice contemplation in the daytime.

Sit cross-legged on a comfortable seat. For a short time, focus the eyes on the sky without moving them. Then one's consciousness becomes clear and lucid. Lower the gaze a little, look straight ahead, and a fresh meditative experience arises. When one recognizes this experience and relaxes in that state, instant presence manifests in its clarity aspect like self-luminous space. This is named "the clear light, of clarity." When one is familiar with that state, one experiences the clear light of clarity where manifestations of perceptual experience and mind arise unified in space beyond concept without interruption.

According to circumstances, experiences sometimes occur such as the thought, "I exist in the space of the sky" or "My body and mind are distinctly separated." At that time, innumerable things manifest, like rainbow lights, *thigles*, and visions of deities. This inherent radiance of the clarity of the five *pranas* is named "the clear light of outer colors."

Through the clear light of outer colors one is able to see clearly the atoms of one's body and the inner organs of one's body. One is able to see visions similar to day and night, the insides of the bodies of others, pure realms, what is being done by sentient beings living in villages, and beings who are dying and reincarnating.

To integrate contemplation with sleep, gently hold *prana*[1] while in the sleeping position of a lion.[2] Without closing the eyes,[3] one falls asleep fixing mind on a radiant sphere of five colors inside one's heart. When external manifestations subside more and more, there exists a brilliant nonconceptual consciousness in that interval between sleep and dream that recognizes the clear light. Falling asleep in that dimension beyond unconscious stupor, sleep arises as clear light.

Moreover, there are no dreams, and consciousness is naturally lucid in the state of contemplation. When one does fall asleep, one has unceasing awareness of all the aspects of forms, sounds, and smells that surround one, and because of that, when one is inexperienced, one is more likely to wake up from this sleep. There is a natural clarity of the manifestation aspect apart from the cessation of judgments about daytime manifestations.

Moreover, with the cessation of the mental consciousness of the six senses, there is unceasing clarity of the sensory consciousnesses of the five sense organs. When mental consciousness dissolves into the clear light, *prana* enters the central channel.[4] Because the five sensory consciousnesses are nonconceptual, they do not become attached to the manifestations. This is named "the clear light of clarity beyond concept."

At this time, with the existence of the condition of the contemplation of the clear light of sensation and the existence of the unceasing manifestations of the clear light of clarity, the clear light beyond concepts naturally exists in that condition free from discursive thoughts. Because of this, when the clear light of the natural ground integrates beyond duality with the natural lucidity of the child in the dimension of primordial purity, deeper clarity manifests in the primordial clarity. This is named "the clear light which integrates mother and child."[5]

Naturally, the clear light of sensation is apparent and abides in unification with spontaneously born joy. The clear light of clarity manifests when contemplation is totally integrated at all times of day and night. And the clear light beyond concepts exists when the mind's acts of conception naturally dissolve. On those occasions, this pattern is clear, so it is easy to understand the meaning. Although it exists at other times, it is difficult to recognize.

As the clear light of sensation abides inseparably from contemplation, the manifestations bring the experience of infinite bliss.

Experiences of the clear light of clarity include manifestations of smoke, mirages, glow, fog, lightning, appearances with five colors, *thigles*, divine figures, sentient beings, and directly seeing many pure realms. One may see through to forms that are blocked by coarse concrete substances, like buildings or mountains, and have the ability to penetrate things like buildings and fences. One may have the unconditioned eye, and various supernormal knowledges.

The clear light beyond concepts totally integrates with contemplation day and night. When any manifestation is viewed, the manifestation dissolves without concepts. Whatever is spoken has no categories and dissolves without concepts, and there manifest all kinds of experiences like the sense of always abiding in the dimension of space.

Here is the method to practice post-contemplation in the day-time. "Post-contemplation" means emerging from contemplation. When one emerges from that state of contemplation, external manifestations are insubstantial aspects of the five colors. Sentient beings, fruit trees, elements, and whatever manifests are seen to be clearly appearing although they are really nothing, just like the reflection of the moon in water. They are seen to be of the nature of the eight examples of illusion. They are seen to be naturally empty like space. Experiencing and integrating with these manifestations, one trains in a state beyond concepts with no attachment to the manifestations of empty clarity.

Here is the method to condense senses to the essential point in the evening. Sit with crossed legs. Visualize a stacked series of white ཨ letters in the central channel from its lower end up to the aperture of Brahma. All those ཨ letters gradually dissolve one into the other from the bottom to the top. They all dissolve into a white ཨ, which is visualized in the small hole at the top of the head. Finally, even that ཨ dissolves in the space of the sky, and one relaxes, freeing mind in that state.

Here is the method to put objects into the vase at midnight. Lie down in the position of the lion. Visualize a lamp of five colors in the center of one's heart, or visualize a radiant white letter ཨ encircled by a *thigle* of five colors. Relax in that condition and fall asleep.

Here is the method to radiate wisdom at dawn. Look straight ahead with the unmoving gaze of the lion. Hold mind in the visualization of a hovering white ཨ in the sky about an arrow's length from the top of the head.

Firstly, one focuses mind on the radiant ཨ, and then one relaxes in that condition so that the ཨ disappears into its own nature.

Although there is no movement of thought, a lucid clarity still manifests, and one relaxes in that state of contemplation.

The root tantra *Dra Thalgyur* summarizes clear light practice:

> With the four outer times the practitioner practices with the physical body. The key is to hold the channels in their source. With the four internal times the practitioner practices with the voice. The key is to interrupt the river of expression. With the four secret times the practitioner practices with the mind. The key is to be familiar with sleep. With the four times of the essential condition after uniting body, voice, and mind one integrates total clear light with sleep. Becoming familiar with these, one unifies with the kayas, practitioner!

CHAPTER 6

Dreams of Clarity

From an early age, Chögyal Namkhai Norbu has had an exceptional capacity for dreamwork. The following three dreams, drawn with permission from his archive, illustrate extraordinary examples of "clarity" within the Dream State.

Dream 1

When I was eight years old, in the twelfth month of the Fire-Dog Year, 1946, I was invited by my maternal uncle[1] Khyentrul Rinpoche Jigdral Thubten Chökyi Gyatso, also known as Jamyang Chökyi Wangchug and Pawo Heka Lingpa. So I traveled to Derge Zulkhog Galing.[2] In the presence of Drubje Lama Rinpoche Kunga Palden,[3] I received the *Yeshe Thongdrol*,[4] the initiation and instructions of the *Kunzang Gongdü* of Padling,[5] and the *Rangdrol Korsum* of Kunkhyen Longchen Rabjampa.[6] From Uncle Rinpoche I also received the transmission of Nyingma Tantras. One night during this time I had the following dream:

There was Uncle Khyentrul Rinpoche together with his disciples Yogi Kunzang Rangdrol,[7] Togden Champa Tendar, and myself. Master and disciples were climbing upward on the slope of a dense forest abounding with different species; after a short time we came upon an east-facing cottage, beautifully adorned with various designs and arrived not too far from the very delightful main door that was something like the form of a radiant rainbow.

At that time Uncle Khyentrul Rinpoche said to us, "Kunkhyen Longchen Rabjampa lives in the upper story of this large house; let us go meet him." We followed Rinpoche and arrived at the door of that house. Then we slowly entered. On the left and right of the steps and the veranda of the house were girls with half naked bodies. Half of their bodies were beautifully adorned with various silk garments, precious jewelry, and bone ornaments. Their facial expressions suggested intoxication with lust. Some of them had orange-red hair, others had shiny black hair hanging loosely. They were walking around in different ways. The moment they saw us, they displayed joy and reverence. They touched together the thumbs to the forefingers and joined their two hands. They displayed a hand mudra with the tips of the two outstretched middle fingers touching, and with the two ring fingers and two little fingers stretched straight out. Uncle Khyentrul Rinpoche replied to them with a mudra in which the thumbs and forefingers of his two hands were connected together like a bracelet, and the middle, ring, and little fingers were stretched out like a little flying bird.

While I was thinking about asking Uncle Khyentrul Rinpoche, "What is the meaning of those mudras?" we reached the downstairs door. There was a magnificent reception hall beautifully decorated with various ornaments. In the middle of the hall about one and a half feet off the ground, was a red triangular altar. On top of this was a green altar with a half-moon shape whose carved opening faced the door, and on top of that was a white circular altar. Each altar was on top of another whose surface size was larger. There were many different kinds of meat—including human flesh—and there was a large collection of various kinds of foods. In the middle of this, a very majestic and towering torma offering had been prepared; this faced the door.

Surrounding that altar, on surfaces formed with many three-tiered triangular platforms about fifteen inches off the ground, there were many yogis and yoginis in sexual embrace whose faces indicated both Tibetan and Indian heritage. They were singing the melody for *a ho ma ha su kha ho*.[8]

As soon as I saw those yogis and yoginis, I was embarrassed and could not bear to examine them in detail. From my embarrassment at that time, I felt like even the hairs on my body were standing up.

We, master and disciples, entered the reception hall. Circling with the assembly on our right side, we slowly went farther along. Suddenly, Uncle Khyentrul Rinpoche began singing an exquisitely beautiful melody that I had never heard before. He sang this vajra song *kol la i re ti am bho la* as if he were the lead singer of the assembly, and he walked along making various dancing movements with his two hands. All the yogis and yoginis included in that assembly, as well as numerous naked girls adorned with silk and bone ornaments and also many male and female attendants, were turning in swinging dance postures while playing different types of musical instruments, some of which I had seen and heard before and some of which were unfamiliar. In unison with Uncle Khyentrul Rinpoche, they sang the same melody of the vajra song *kol la i re ti* in one voice. The song concluded with *din di ma ta hi na badza dzi a i* and once again, like before, the assembly repeated the beautiful melody of *a ho ma ha su kha ho* many times.

After quite a while, the half-naked girls adorned with silk and bone ornaments began to distribute feast substances to the yogis and yoginis one after another.

We arrived in front of the great torma offering, and a girl with brilliant, luminous blue hair, dressed in bone ornaments, offered to Uncle Khyentrul Rinpoche a skull cup full of feast alcohol with her right hand and a *kapala* full of feast offerings with her left hand. She was singing this song with a beautiful melody:

> See everything here as beautiful; those assembled here have no doubt; enjoy with the knowledge that Brahmin, outcast, dog, and pig have the same nature.

Uncle Khyentrul Rinpoche made the lotus mudra and then received the *kapala* of feast offerings with his right hand and the *kapala* of feast alcohol with his left hand while saying *a la la ho*. Three girls offered the three of us the feast offerings and feast alcohol, and we received them, imitating Uncle Rinpoche.

While we were enjoying the feast offerings, I noticed there was a small piece of human forefinger together with the fingernail in my *kapala* of feast offerings. As soon as I saw this, something like nausea arose, and I was not able to enjoy the feast offerings. I asked Rinpoche to look at the human forefinger, saying, "Rinpoche, please look here. Is this not a human forefinger?"

Uncle Rinpoche just smiled and replied, "Did you not understand the meaning of the song when we just now received the feast substances offered by the dakinis?" I had read the song for offering the feast substances many times, and though the words were present in my mind, until now there had never been a reason to give any thought to their meaning. Although I immediately gave some thought to the meaning of the words, I still could not precisely understand their meaning. I recalled other times, when I offered some Ganapujas together with Togden Rinpoche. Togden Rinpoche said to me, "It is very important and necessary to enjoy everything, whatever there is, without making a distinction between good and bad." After I understood the meaning of what he had said those times, I ate some things from the feast substances, but I still refrained from eating that human forefinger, although I drank all the feast alcohol.

While we enjoyed the feast substances, in front of us, on top of a platform about a foot and a half high, a yogi with very long, black, braided hair and adorned with many bone ornaments on his mostly naked body was copulating in a standing position with a naked yogini also adorned with bone ornaments. The *yab* was offering feast offerings to the *yum* and the *yum* was offering feast alcohol to the *yab*. Remaining like that, the *yab yum* pair turned their faces toward Uncle Rinpoche. Smiling and happy, the feast substances of the *yab* were put into the right hand of the *yum*, and the feast alcohol of the *yum* was put into the left hand of the *yab*. Then the right hand of the *yab* and the left hand of the *yum* made the mudra at the heart with the thumb and forefinger of the hand touching. Uncle Khyentrul Rinpoche replied with the mudra of both his hands held at the heart with thumbs and forefingers touching.

I asked Uncle Khyentrul Rinpoche, "Who are these two *yab yum* practitioners?" Uncle Khyentrul Rinpoche replied, "These two practitioners are Ngadag Nyang Ral[9] *yab yum.*" When he said that, the three of us were filled with devotion, and we offered the mudra in imitation of Rinpoche.

Then Uncle Khyentrul Rinpoche went to the second floor, and we followed after him. We went inside through the eastern door of that reception hall. There were doors on each of the east, south, and west sides of that very magnificent eight-sided reception hall. There was a calm atmosphere inside the hall. The walls were rainbow-colored with transparent stained-glass windows. In the middle of this, inside a tent of *thigles* of light, was a yogi with white garments who wore a crown of his long hair fastened to his head. When I was very little, Uncle Togden Rinpoche[10] gave to me a small painting of Rigdzin Jigmed Lingpa, which had been a practice support of Adzom Drugpa Rinpoche.[11] The shape of the yogi's body and garments were very similar in all respects to the painting.

All around that great *thigle* tent there were many different types of people, such as yogis and yoginis with Tantric clothes, naked people with bone ornaments, those with the aspect of male and female attendants, those with a style of dress unfamiliar to me, as well as those with the clothing of ordinary men and women. In between all these there were many wearing the dress of ordained men and women.

When we entered into that reception hall, everyone in there sang in unison a very beautiful melody of *ha ha sha sa ma.*[12] The six letters were sung over and over. When we went inside, Uncle Rinpoche began singing together with them and circled the reception hall in a clockwise direction. We also went along imitating Rinpoche. Finally, master and students completed the inner circumambulation and arrived once again at the location of the eastern door.

At that time, Uncle Khyentrul Rinpoche looked for a brief instant with unmoving eyes directly at the yogi in the middle of the *thigle* tent and held the palms of his two hands joined at his heart. The yogi in the middle of the *thigle* tent looked with his eyes directly at Uncle Rinpoche and, with a smiling face, he displayed a mudra by arranging his two hands so that the two thumbs were touching the two forefingers, and he put together the two tips of his two extended middle fingers; the ring finger and the little finger separated and extended straight out. When his eyes leisurely gazed into space without moving, a girl dressed with bone ornaments arrived who had at her heart a clear, polished, thumb-sized silver mirror, in the center of which was the letter *ca* as a golden symbolic letter. She asked Uncle Rinpoche to sit on the seat in front of that great *thigle* tent, and immediately Uncle Rinpoche went there and sat down. I went together with Uncle Rinpoche and sat on a seat on the left side of him. Immediately, when Uncle Rinpoche sat on the seat, the yogi in the middle of the *thigle* tent joined the thumbs and fingers of his two hands, opened his middle, ring, and little fingers, and rested them on his knees. Smiling with happiness, the yogi sang the very beautiful melody of the Song of the Vajra *e ma ki ri ki ri*.[13] Since he sang slowly with a fine supple voice, absolutely everybody there joined in the singing with one melodious voice until *ra ra ra*.

During all of that time, I was like a newborn infant without thoughts, like a mute who could not speak. My body trembled and pulsated a little. I was in a state of *hadewa* and it was not possible to define my feelings. Each successive *ra* of the *ra ra ra* at the end of the song was sung louder and louder by the entire assembly in unison, and that final *ra* was shouted more powerfully than the roar of a thousand simultaneous thunderclaps. Under those circumstances, I woke up.

That was the first time I heard the Song of the Vajra. From then on I remembered it clearly. The song always arises clearly in my mind, and sometimes I spontaneously hear that beautiful melody.

That morning when I went to see Uncle Rinpoche, I related the vivid details about how this dream manifested in me. Uncle Rinpoche said, "That is a marvelous sign of entering the empowering flow of the lineage," and he was very, very happy. He went to get a notebook to record how I related the dream, and later when I was older, he gave it to me to refresh my memory.

I asked Uncle Rinpoche, "What is this mantra *e ma ki ri ki ri?*" After I asked that question, he explained to me that it was the Song of the Vajra and, in connection with that, he kindly gave me a simple empowerment and instructions on Liberation by Wearing, which are in the *Lama Gongdü*.[14]

Then I asked Uncle Rinpoche, "Please teach me the melody for the Song of the Vajra."

Uncle Rinpoche replied, "For sure, there is a definitive melody for the Song of the Vajra. But I do not know it. What was the melody like, which you heard in your dream? Look, can you sing a little of the melody?" He persistently encouraged me like this. When I repeated the little that I remembered, Uncle Rinpoche was very pleased.

Uncle Rinpoche said, "I heard that there is a way of singing the Song of the Vajra at Adzomgar. You should ask Drokhe Togden,[15] probably he will know it."

Later when I met with Togden Rinpoche, I asked him to tell me the customary melody for the Song of the Vajra as sung at Adzomgar. Togden Rinpoche said, "Kyabje Drugpa Rinpoche now and then sang this Song of the Vajra. But I do not know a specific melody for the song at the Gar other than what was sung experientially by Drugpa Rinpoche himself. But I remember that it was sung like this by Drugpa Rinpoche." After saying that, he sang a little bit of the melody. At a later meeting, the melody of the Song of the Vajra contained in the text of the *Shitro Khorde Rangdrol Gyi Tagdrol* revealed by my root master Changchub Dorje[16] was mostly the same as what was sung by Togden Rinpoche.

Then I asked Uncle Rinpoche, "Do you know the melody of *kol la i re ti*, which I heard in my dream?" Uncle Rinpoche replied, "What is that melody? See if you can sing a little bit." I bravely sang the little of the song I could remember. Uncle Rinpoche said, "Yes, that's it; one time in a dimension that mixed dream and meditation experience, I went to the country of Oddiyana and met the great Rigdzin Jampal Shenyen.[17] Many dakas and dakinis were offering a Ganachakra, and about seven times they sang the very beautiful melody of *kol la i re ti*. And another time, in a dream in the place Tsariti, and another time in the place Dewikoti,[18] I also went to a Ganachakra of dakas and dakinis; and I sang this song with them on many occasions: *kol la i re ti*; the melody was the same as that without any change. Without any doubt, you definitely met with dakas and dakinis from a special place like Oddiyana; it's really good." He was very pleased.

I asked Uncle Rinpoche, "By all means, please teach me what you know of the melody of *kol la i re ti*," and I was very insistent. Uncle Rinpoche promised, "I'm uncertain and don't know that melody exactly; but as you wish, what I do know we two will practice together quietly." Later, when I was twelve years old in the middle of the first month of spring in the Iron-Tiger Year, while traveling with my uncle in the lower part of Kham Kyegu, Uncle Rinpoche kindly practiced with me the melody of *kol la i re ti* together with some special secret instructions connected with it.

Dream 2

I was fifteen years old; it was in the middle of the second of the two months of the double fifth month of the Water-Snake Year,

1953. I was on retreat in Gyawo Ritröd[19] of Trokhog in Derge in Dokham. On the twenty-fifth day while I was receiving the initiation and instructions of *Dzogchen Nyingthig Yazhi*[20] from my Uncle Khyentrul Rinpoche, master and disciples together offered a long Ganapuja of *Khandro Nyingthig*[21] in the evening; and in the early morning I had a dream.

While I was in the great cave of Gyawo Ritröd, suddenly a beautiful girl adorned with jewel ornaments entered through the cave door. I thought she might be the green dakini who abided on the right side of Pal Lhamo[22] at the time when I saw the five dakinis in one of my previous dreams. She gave me a very small, yellow scroll and said with a subtle, sweet voice, "Pal Lhamo gives this to you."

Very surprised, I quickly accepted the yellow scroll with my left hand, and I asked, "Who are you?" But the girl disappeared. I immediately opened the little yellow scroll and looked carefully. On the scroll there was nothing other than three letters very similar to the Tibetan *uchen*[23] letters *a*, *hu*, and *ma*, written in vermilion color. At that time, I was thinking about what *tertön* Nyima Pal[24] told me when I met him in a dream when I was in Sengchen Namdrag.[25] According to what he explained, I understood that the terma letters more or less manifest from the symbolic letters. Immediately I invoked Ekajati, and when I looked at the three letters on the yellow scroll, infinite light rays emanated from those three letters. Although there was something like clusters of very small letters in the dust of the light rays, apart from recognizing them to be letters and reading a few, they did not manifest clearly. I was afraid to lose the scroll, so I held it in my left hand, and I tightly held my left hand with my right hand because I felt it was necessary to offer this to Uncle Rinpoche. I woke up in that condition.

As soon as I woke up, I very clearly remembered the dream and noticed that my left hand was tightly held just like in my dream. I opened my left hand to look, and I could physically feel that the little scroll was there. But since it was not yet dawn, I again held it tightly in my left hand, and I stayed still like this waiting for dawn. After about a half an hour it was dawn, so I got up from my bed. When the light of dawn arrived at the entrance of the cave, I looked carefully at the yellow scroll in my hand. It was transparent and the width of a finger. Its length was about four inches and the three letters *a*, *hu*, and *ma* were written in reddish vermilion. Immediately, I put on my clothes, walked to the door of Uncle Rinpoche's cave, and knocked on his door.

Rinpoche said, "I haven't completed my morning practice yet. Why have you come so early like this?" After telling the story, I put the yellow scroll into his hand; he examined it carefully and said, "Ah, what an auspicious occasion! Last year I saw these three symbolic letters on a terma list of a Vajrapani statue from the place of Lhalung Paldor.[26] I have been waiting for this yellow scroll to arrive for a long time. And now it is very good that it arrives in your hand."

Taking a text from the bookshelf behind him, he showed me how it had been written that there existed a very clear indication of how these symbolic letters of Lhalung Sangdag would occur. I then offered those symbolic letters to Uncle Rinpoche, requesting that he give me the cycle of teachings of Lhalung Sangdag, and receiving his promise that he would give them.

Dream 3

When I was twenty-two years old, in the early part of April of the Iron-Mouse Year, 1960, during the day I was at a nice hotel near the mountain Gransasso in Italy. Alone and on foot, I climbed the mountain, and I arrived on top of a high rock cliff. For about an hour I experienced the Dzogchen Upadesha *Semdzin* named Struggle of the Asuras[27] and, after that, while I was practicing *namkha arted*,[28] a totally resplendent great eye manifested vividly and clearly in the expanse of the pure sky. I looked directly at it and relaxed in the condition of absolute equality where manifestation and mind are nondual. In the middle of the eye, a golden luminescent symbolic letter similar to *bam* shone clearly for about a minute. Then the vision disappeared the way a rainbow dissolves in the sky. I had the following dream in the early morning.

I was in a park near Wöntöd Lobdra[29] in Derge in Dokham, reading Vimala's commentary on the *Namasangiti*.[30] I was thinking about how I wanted to ask for explanation and guidance about Vimala's commentary when I went to see my lama Rinpoche Khyenrab Ödser.[31] In that moment, Tsewang Phüntsog[32] of Lhadrong[33] monastery was coming in my direction. I asked him, "Shall the two of us go before Lama Rinpoche to request explanation and guidance on Vimala's commentary on the *Namasangiti*?"

Tsewang said, "Didn't you know that Lama Rinpoche has died?"

In response to that, I asked, "I didn't know this. When did he die?"

"Five months have passed since Lama Rinpoche died."

"Did he die in his house at the college?"

"No, he died in Derge Gönchen."[34]

Then I asked, "Where are the remains of Lama Rinpoche?"

"They are somewhere in Derge Gönchen; but I am not certain exactly where."

I immediately went with him to look inside the college. But we did not see anyone inside the college other than two old, Böntöd monks of the meditation hall. I asked those two old monks, "Where did all the college students go?"

Despairingly, one monk said, "I cannot say they went there or here; they all dispersed, just like little birds are scattered by a hawk."

I asked Tsewang Phüntsog, "Should the two of us go see the remains of Lama Rinpoche?"

He said, "It's okay to go."

I said, "Well let us go right now."

The two of us set out on foot for Derge from Böntöd. Along the way, we frequently met Chinese and Tibetan people dressed in

Chinese clothes. Sometimes we passed by them without giving it much thought, and sometimes we kept hidden. Finally, we arrived at Derge Gönchen. Gönchen was completely full of Chinese and Tibetan people dressed in Chinese clothes. We arrived by the stupa near the edge of the monastery, and there we met an old woman. I asked the old woman, "Have you ever met Böntöd Khen Rinpoche Khyenrab?"

She said, "I met him. He is my root master."

Then I asked, "Where is he now?"

Laughing, she said, "I don't know where he is now, but his remains are in Black Water."[35]

I asked her, "We are the master's students, so will you explain how we can see the master's remains?"

She said, "Well, you must come here at dusk this evening."

So until dusk that evening we remained hidden in the innermost part of the ground floor of the stupa of the five families. As soon as it was dusk, we went to Black Water with the old woman. We arrived beside a boulder, and the old woman looked around everywhere and said, "The remains of Lama Rinpoche were placed there. But I don't know whether they have been taken to another dimension by the dakinis or eaten by dogs or stolen by humans. Now we cannot see them. How sad!" After saying that she returned home.

We sat near the boulder and chanted several invocations to the Lama. Then, saying, "I will investigate whether the lama's remains are around here," Tsewang Phüntsog went off. I sat in that place without moving, and through Guruyoga I remained in nondual integration of primordial mind and ordinary mind. Suddenly, right in front of me was a black woman with braided hair; she wore black clothes on her body and was repulsive. She asked, "Are you searching for the remains of Lama Khyenrab Rinpoche?"

In response I asked, "Yes, but the remains are not here. Do you know where the remains are?"

She said, "Since the material remains are integrated in the dimension of the elements, it is not possible to see them now. The immaterial remains of the essence of the elements are in the great tomb of the *rigdzins* and dakinis."

Then I asked her, "Can you direct me to the great tomb of the *rigdzins* and dakinis?"

She said, "I can. Come now."

I asked, "I need to wait here a little for Tsewang Phüntsog. Is it okay if we go as soon as he arrives?"

She said, "If we wait for Tsewang Phüntsog to arrive, it will not be possible to go. If you want to go, we must leave now."

At that time, from not very far away, quite a few Chinese and Tibetans in Chinese clothes were coming in our direction. This created a bristling fear in my mind. Then, as soon as that black woman made a sudden sound by clapping her hands, there was darkness, and I could not see.

The woman said to me, "It is not necessary to be afraid."

I thought how I was saved from the hands of those Chinese and Tibetans in Chinese clothes. Delighted, I had no fear in the darkness. After a little while the black woman took my hand and said, "Come here now."

I went a little farther in the direction she led me, and we passed through a door and arrived inside. There was a delightful, charming scene with a majestic courtyard with four great gates in the four directions. We went toward the great gate near us, arrived in front of it, and went inside. Inside, there was a very high stupa in the middle of a square. There were thirteen terraced steps all around its golden peak that glowed with resplendent light. Lined up side by side on top of all of those steps were many hundreds of large and small enlightenment stupas.

The black woman said, "Now we go on top of the sixth step, which is where the remains of Khen Khyenrab Ödser Rinpoche are located." Right away she left and came to a place with the sixth tier on her left side. She pointed her forefinger at a stupa and said, "This stupa has the remains of Khen Khyenrab Ödser Rinpoche." The two of us arrived before the stupa and, showing me the treasure door of the stupa, she said, "Look here. Behind the treasure door is the essential body of the remains of Lama Khyenrab Ödser Rinpoche." I looked carefully at them. In there was the body of Khen Khyenrab Ödser Rinpoche, about a finger's width in size. His body was like something made from the pure essence of the five lights. His sense organs were pure with great radiance. His two dazzling eyes were looking at me, but he did not speak. That is what I saw.

At that time I was very sad and I cried out, "Lama Rinpoche. May your compassion unfailingly help me." I said this with urgency. The black woman said, "You should not allow intense sorrow like that. After Khen Khyenrab Ödser Rinpoche remains in undistracted contemplation as a body of luminous essences for twenty-one human years, he will again take a human body to benefit the teachings and beings."

I wanted to ask many questions like "In what place will he be reborn," but I was awakened from sleep by some noise.

CHAPTER 7

The Methods of Transference[1]

The explanation of how to practice the essence of transference has three subdivisions, pertaining to the method of transference for those of higher, middle, and lower capacity.

The first is the explanation of the method of transference from the clear light for those of higher capacity. In this context, when a male or female practitioner has really mastered the clear light in him or herself, at the moment of death, from that realm of the clear light that has previously been mastered, *rigpa* comes out from the aperture of Brahma and transfers into the space of primordial being.

Then there is the explanation of the method of transference from the illusory body for those of medium capacity. In this case, when there is sufficient proficiency with illusory body in the context of the mind stream of male and female practitioners, at the moment of death, from the dimension of illusory body, *rigpa* shoots from the aperture of Brahma. It is then transferred to the form of a deity of the real condition. The illusory body of the bardo is thus recognized, and one becomes enlightened.

The third is the explanation of the method of transference from body and voice for those of lower capacity, which can be understood in the section on preliminary practices of the innermost Upadesha teachings. Transference from body, voice, and mind can be summarized into the fundamental principles said to be the two types of concrete transference in accord with actions of channels and chakras and elements of interdependent origination, and insubstantial transference in accord with the power of visualization of mind.[2]

CHAPTER 8

The Pilgrimage to Maratika

In 1984, Chögyal Namkhai Norbu traveled to northern Nepal on a pilgrimage to the monastery of Tolu and to the cave of Maratika[1] where the great Mahasiddha[2] Padmasambhava[3] did a retreat with his consort Mandarava.[4] The following is an account of a series of remarkable dreams he had on this trip, beginning with a dream he had two days after reaching the monastery.

The location of the dream was Tolu Monastery itself. If you dream about a place or a thing where you have been in the past, this usually reflects a repetition through karmic trace; if you dream of a place or a situation where you are not and have not been, this reflects a desire or a wish. On the other hand, if you dream of the place where you actually are, this is often significant. Thus, I was clued that this might be an important dream.

In this dream, I was at the cave of Tolu, and even the people who had actually accompanied me on the trip were there. As I was teaching my students, my uncle joined us. I should tell you that this man who joined us was not only my uncle; he was also one of my principal teachers and an extraordinary practitioner and tertön.[5]

I will tell you a short story to illustrate the remarkable quality of my uncle's life. When I was a child, I was living near a monastery. At the time I am recalling, a young horse had died. Vultures had eaten the horse, but even after they had finished, one of the vultures remained. My uncle asked two of the monks to go and fetch this vulture.

Upon their return to the monastery with the vulture, the monks announced that the bird had been wounded. There was a piece of iron lodged in its shoulder. One of the monks attempted to pull it out, but the vulture became quite agitated. My uncle instructed this monk to stop and to put the vulture in an enclosed garden area. I remember thinking how strange it was that the vulture would remain so silent and passive while this was occurring. In fact, the whole situation was becoming more and more unusual.

The next day, my uncle instructed me to feed the vulture some milk. When I arrived at the garden, which was semicircular in shape, with a wooden floor and a covering over it, the vulture was sitting immobile. I placed the milk before it. Moving its head slightly it began to drink. It drank up all of the milk I had offered, and when it had finished, began to run, and as it did so, moved its wings slightly. As the area was quite long, it was able to run a long distance. It ran clear to the end of the garden and then halfway back. Then it stopped, and the metal piece, an iron rod, dropped from its wing. The very moment the iron piece fell out, the vulture flew away, heading due east in the direction of a large mountain called Sitang. The famous Dzogchen Monastery[6] is behind that mountain. It was also on that mountain that my uncle normally lived in a cave.

We examined the iron piece that had fallen from the vulture's wing; it was quite long. The top that had been embedded in the wing was triangular. I can still remember the beautiful sound that the iron piece made when it fell from the wing. This event was merely one of the oddities that frequently occurred around my uncle.

So, on that occasion at Tolu, my uncle manifested within my dream. In the dream he was no older than fourteen or fifteen years of age. He said to me that he was very pleased that I was

giving such a beautiful teaching and that it was useful to everyone. I asked him if he had really been listening. He replied that
he had heard every word. What I had been teaching at Tolu was
the *Tsigsum Nedeg*,[7] the famous three final statements of Garab
Dorje.[8] Then my uncle asked me to explain about my *gongter*[9]
also. I replied that the *namkha*[10] was not a *gongter*.

Allow me to explain to what I was referring. A few years ago,
I was in New York City. I was giving a seminar about the function
of elements and energy, as well as about Tibetan history. At this
seminar, I gave an explanation of the elements and their functioning according to the ancient Bönpo tradition. That night I had a
dream. In it there was a small boy dressed in blue. I asked him
who he was, and he replied that his name was Phuwer.[11] Phuwer
was a famous Bönpo deity particularly known for his capacity to
accomplish divination through astrology.

I said, "If you are really Phuwer, then explain to me about the
function of the elements of individuals and how one might harmonize them when there are problems." This small child then
proceeded to explain the different kinds of functions of the elements, relating to body, life, fortune, capacity, etc. Through this
I discovered the precise principle of *namkha*, the method of har-
monizing the elements of a person.

I had said that the *namkha* was not a *gongter* but simply the
result of that dream, but he insisted that because it was a *gongter*,
he would like a transmission. Insofar as he is my teacher, I didn't
really feel comfortable with his request, but he insisted, and so
eventually I did read him the book and thus gave the transmission.

After that was complete, he said that the *namkha* will be an
important practice in the future. He also said that I must practice
and teach on the "five dakinis practice." I asked what this "five
dakinis practice" is. He responded that there would be some indi-
cations later. That was one of my dreams.

During the days we spent at Tolu Monastery, I had extremely
important dreams constantly, and by the time we approached the

astrologically significant twenty-fifth day,[12] I was a bit nervous about sleeping. With a concern as to what would happen now, I went to bed, but for quite a while I couldn't sleep. Finally, when I did sleep, I found myself in a kind of dream in which I was speaking with someone. I actually don't know if I was speaking with someone else or carrying on a conversation with myself.

The voice instructed me to relax, first the breathing, and then the body, until I found myself in the relaxed state of Samaya.[13] I thought to myself that I had never heard of this relaxed state of Samaya. Nevertheless, I tried again and again to relax, and to put myself into that state. Each time, largely due to my discomfort with the sleeping conditions at Tolu, I would wake up. Indeed, I awoke at least two or three times in the course of trying to get into the state of relaxation. On one of these occasions, I received instructions within the dream to loosen the mountaineering leggings that, due to exhaustion, I had failed to remove before falling asleep.

When I awoke, remembering the instructions, I untied them, and fell asleep once again, slowly relaxing into the state of Samaya. "It's not perfect yet," the voice said, "we have to have fresher, easier breathing." In order to comply, I opened the tent to let in some fresh air, even though it was very cold and a fierce wind was blowing. Once again I returned to sleep and entered Samaya. I was again thinking that this Samaya wasn't that terrific, not really a state of contemplation.[14]

The voice returned and said, "Now that you've done that, you have to get to the state of Dharmadhatu."[15] As instructed, I relaxed and directed myself toward this state of Dharmadhatu. Shortly, I was awakened by a cough from a nearby tent.

I went back to sleep yet another time, and directed myself to go through the successive levels of relaxation. Again and again I awoke for one reason or another and had to start from the beginning. Then suddenly the voice was saying, "We're here, this is the state of Dharmadhatu," which seemed to me to be the state of contemplation.

The voice now instructed me to direct myself to another state. As I did this, there began to appear a kind of *thigle*[16] similar to one that had appeared in a previous dream at Tolu cave. I also saw some writing, and then I woke up once again...

I had to start at the beginning, relaxing through the different stages until the *thigle* reappeared. What I had seen in the *thigle* was the title of a text. This time, after the title, there appeared a text itself, just as if I were looking at a movie screen. One after another, an entire series of meditation practices appeared. I was reading page after page, but if at any point I couldn't read one, I would only need to think to myself that this wasn't clear, and the unclear portion would return. It would repeat itself as if I had some sort of telecommand. In this manner I read the whole text from beginning to end at least three or four times.

Due to interruptions, I awoke frequently. But each time I would go back to sleep, and begin with Samaya and all the rest, and then the text would go on.

Suddenly the voice said, "You are now in the next state." What distinguished this state from the previous one was that now the few words that had not been completely clear appeared to occupy all of space. Without any focusing or staring on my part, they just appeared. Thus I went on reading, and this continued without interruption almost until morning.

At this point I coughed intensely and awoke. The words were still there even with my eyes open. It wasn't a dream. I saw them for a short time, and then they disappeared. I thought that perhaps this was just the influence of the dream. Curious, I continued to look into the sky. The sky was very clear, and there was no more vision.

I remembered one time when I was doing a retreat in Norway. I was in the middle of a practice when the same thing happened.

I told some people about my experience at that time. Previously, I had read about *nangwa yiger shar*[17] in the biographies of some accomplished teachers. In Norway, I recall having thought that I had not previously understood what the phrase *nangwa yiger shar* means. Anyway, I fell asleep once again, and relaxed through the successive stages. In the dream, while being instructed to enter the various states of relaxation, I suddenly had a thought about an even further state—something entitled *chadrub yeshe*, all-accomplishing wisdom. The voice answered my thought, saying, "It will come when all is completed." Then morning came. I was truly exhausted. Everyone else was still pleasantly asleep. That is the story of the twenty-fifth day.

The next day, we had a long climb. That evening, when I fell asleep, it all happened again. Again I read the text through several times, particularly the areas where the letters hadn't been sharp. At a certain point, I suddenly woke up. I found my head covered with a blanket. There had been so much wind that I must have been protecting myself. Uncovering my head, I opened my eyes, and immediately looked into the sky. There, very briefly, were the letters again.

I'd like to tell you now about a dream I had on the first night that we arrived at Maratika cave. Before going to bed, I thought to myself that tomorrow would be a good day to begin a long-life meditation practice that I had brought along. I still hadn't entirely developed a particular method for doing this practice, but I had carried the practice text along with me because I had had the idea that Maratika would be a nice place to practice it.

That night I dreamed that I was preparing to do the practice in a big cave. I was explaining how the practice would be done, and was giving an initiation, which would enable the students to do the practice themselves. Normally, in our tradition, in order to do a long-life practice, one needs a long-life initiation.

Those of you who know me, know that I am not the type who

typically does elaborate formal initiations,[18] but I have always said that it is necessary to do some kind of initiation for empowering. In my dream, I had the idea that I would first give a careful explanation of the meaning of the initiation. When the people had understood it well, I would give empowerment with the mantra. After that, we would do the practice together; that would constitute the voice transmission.

So, in my dream I was explaining each point of what the initiation was, starting with the initiation of the body. At that moment, I noticed that there was a person near to me giving me something. I turned to him and saw that he was not a normal human being. Of this I was certain because the first thing I observed while looking at him was that the lower part of his body was that of a serpent. I thought that perhaps this was Rahula,[19] one of the guardians, but when I looked at his face this seemed unlikely. I then thought that perhaps it was, or represented, someone that I knew. I looked again—his face was dragon-like in appearance. His body was white. Suddenly he placed something into my hand.

If you have taken an initiation, you know that there is usually someone assisting the teacher by giving him things. At the appropriate point in the ceremony, the assistant offers the correct object. In my dream, the dragon-like being was giving me a round object with which I was about to authenticate the initiation of the body that I had just given.

I took the round object into my hand. It was a mirror, but on the rim surrounding the mirror were what seemed to be twelve smaller mirrors. Around them all was a kind of rainbow. And around this perimeter were peacock feathers. It was very beautiful. As I took it into my hand, I knew that this was the object with which I could give the initiation of the body.

Normally in an initiation, the mirror represents the mind, the aspect of understanding. Immediately in the dream, an explanation came to me: "The body seems to be substantial, but inherently it is void. The symbol of this is the reflection that appears to be our form in the mirror." Conveying this explanation, I used the mirror in my dream to give the initiation of the body. In my dream, I touched the mirror to the heads of each of the people receiving initiation. As each went past I also said a mantra.[20]

I next began to explain the initiation of the voice. At this very moment, I sensed the presence of another being on my left. This being also offered an object for authentication. The object was a mala.[21] made of deeply colored red rubies shaped into a figure eight. I looked carefully at the being who was offering the mala. It had a dark red body and only one eye. I thought again that this was no ordinary human being, perhaps it was Ekajati.[22] On the other hand, it didn't seem quite like Ekajati, and in her hands were these strange objects. In any case, just after she gave me the mala, I found that I was again giving an explanation: "This mala represents the continual utterance of the mantra." Not only did I explain the function of mantra but I also gave a very unusual explanation about this form of mantra, which is presented in the form of a figure eight. It was all quite strange because the explanation had nothing to do with the particular long-life practice (*Tsedrub Gongdü*) of Nyagla Pema Dündul[23] with which I had arrived.

The next day, after dreaming about another long-life practice featuring the dakini Mandarava, I discovered that there is really a *yangti* practice that in fact includes this visualization. Meanwhile, the Ekajati figure had placed another object in my hand, this one a symbol for empowering the initiation of mind. The object resembled a swastika, but at the top there were tridents. It was the center that was the swastika. It was constructed of a transparent, precious blue stone.

I then explained the meaning of the initiation of mind. Afterward, I put this object at the heart of each person in turn. At the same time, I was pronouncing the mantra related to initiation of mind. After I placed the object at the first person's heart, I saw that it left an impression and that the impression of the object was turning with a small sound. It seemed very alive. When I initiated the next person the same thing happened. When I was finally finished, I saw that all the swastika impressions were still turning. That was how I conducted the initiation, and then I awoke. The next day I decided to do a retreat inside the cave. Many of the students who accompanied me on this pilgrimage joined me to do the practice of Pema Dündul in the cave of Mandarava.

The next day, I had yet another special dream. Although many of our people had not actually arrived yet, I dreamed that we were all together in the cavern. We had already done a practice together, and I was giving teachings. In the dream it seemed as if the dream of the previous night had been recreated exactly. At my left there was the figure that was dark reddish brown with one eye. Once again, she was holding many objects in her hand; this time she gave me a bead of crystal.

It was now clear that this being was assisting me as I gave instruction. I took the crystal into my hand and looked at it. At the center of the crystal I saw a word. As soon as I saw that special word, I knew that this being was indeed Ekajati. I also had a very clear dream vision of the guardian Ekajati who advised me, saying, "This is the time to open your mind treasure of Life's Circle of Vajra, the dakini practice for obtaining long-life."

Looking inside the small crystal ball, I could see light rays radiating in all directions from the word, but they did not radiate outside the ball. As I took the ball, I asked, "What is this thing?" She said, "This is *tagtheb*. You have to do *tagtheb*." "I don't understand," I replied. The moment I said that, it seemed as if the crystal disappeared inside me. I looked around to see Ekajati, but she too had disappeared.

Upon awakening, my first thought was "*tagtheb*" and what it could mean. It was still far from dawn, I had a lot of time, so I continued to concentrate on the word *tagtheb*. This is not a familiar word. *Tag* means "pure," *theb* means "to confront," or sometimes it means "to list." In my half-awake state I was thinking of this word, when it came to me that what was required was that I write down the text and, later, write it again without referring to the first version in order to test its authenticity. It was now perfectly clear what must be done.

After washing myself, I took a paper and pen, and went out onto a rock. Then, without a plan, I wrote whatever came to my mind. I wrote several pages, and what emerged was an invocation of Ekajati. This was the beginning. Afterward I went to have breakfast. During breakfast, I asked one of my students to fetch me a notebook. When I had finished breakfast, she still had not returned, so I took another notebook to a specific place where I had been on the first day, a power location of Maratika, and sat down.

I had almost begun when the student arrived with a black notebook and a red pen. With these I started writing. It was as if I was starting a letter. I headed it Maratika, along with the hour and the day. It was 9:15 in the morning. While I was writing, various people from my group came over. Some of them didn't know what I was doing. As they came over to greet me, I tried to get rid of them.

Despite interruptions, I finished writing at 12:15. When I had finished, I had used up the last page, right up to the last line of the notebook. It almost seemed as if it had been deliberately planned. I reflected to myself that this was a good sign.

Returning to our campsite, I gave the text to two students to hold for several days. I was thinking that after a few days I would write it out again. That would be the *tagtheb*, the second version to be compared with the first in order to confirm its authenticity. This would be proof that the text was genuine and not merely my intellect at play.

Two days passed. On the third day, I had a dream indicating that the time had come to write and make some clarifications. After completing morning practice, I again sat down to write, and continued until lunchtime. The second time, I wrote it out very calmly in an easy script. This time it took me two and one-half hours. I then asked that the original be returned and that my older sister compare the two versions. There was virtually no difference, only two or three grammatical corrections.

This is the story of the origin of that practice text, a practice for developing a long and firm life. The text includes mantras, exercises for breathing and control of one's energy, as well as visualization. There are also instructions pertaining to chakras and channels. In the Tibetan tradition this type of terma is often sealed, meaning that it has to be kept secret for many, many years. When you are keeping such a thing secret, you are not permitted even to say that you are keeping something secret. In this case, it has not been necessary. There has been no indication that this should be sealed. I have no secret to keep; therefore, I have talked about it. I also talked about it at Maratika, and have done transmission of the mantras.

CHAPTER 9

An Interview with
Chögyal Namkhai Norbu

MICHAEL: I would like to ask you a few questions about dreams. First of all, what is the history of the dream practice that you do?

CHÖGYAL NAMKHAI NORBU: What do you mean "history"?

M: When and by whom was the first dream practice taught? Who was famous for teaching it?

N: It is not easy to answer this because dream teachings come from different kinds of tantra teachings, particularly the *Mahamaya Tantra*, but also from Dzogchen teachings.

M: When was the *Mahamaya Tantra* written?

N: Beyond time; you cannot say when it was written.

M: Was there any particular author?

N: (laughing) There is no author of Tantric teachings. Maybe a mahasiddha transmitted this teaching and introduced it from Oddiyana[1] in India. After all, Saraha introduced the *Guhyasamaja Tantra*, and Tilopa introduced the *Chakrasamvara Tantra*. It is possible that something like that can be said to be the history of the transmission of a tantra, but there is no original history of the tantras.

M: Rinpoche, sometimes you have taught dream practices where one visualizes a white syllable ༀ[2] at the heart, but at other times you have taught that one should visualize an ༀ at the throat. What are the different conditions in which one should visualize the ཨ at one's heart or throat?

N: The visualization of ཨ at the throat is particularly suited for remembering dreams. The visualization of ཨ at the throat has the function of controlling energy and clarity. When you visualize a white ཨ at the heart, you are working with the principle of natural light; that is another method.

M: Why do we dream?

N: Well, sometimes dreaming is due to *pagchag*, the impressions of the day. These include our anxieties, attitudes, and preoccupations. There is also another type of dream that arises from our clarity. This type of dream is dependent on the dreamer's circumstances and clarity.

M: How do we distinguish between dreams that arise from our clarity and dreams that arise from our daily impressions and *pagchag*?

N: If we have had an exhausting day, and all we can do is eat and fall into a heavy sleep, it is not likely that we will have a dream of clarity. More often, in such circumstances, we have dreams about something with which we are preoccupied. It may even be somewhat difficult to remember our dreams due to the heaviness of sleep. On the other hand, as we approach the early morning and are almost at the point of awakening, our dreams may become quite clear. It is more likely that they will be associated with our clarity during this period. If a dream is associated with clarity, it may have special meaning for our lives. It may indicate many things.

M: Is this true also for someone who practices dream yoga?

N: If you are a practitioner of dream yoga, dreams arising out of clarity will develop and increase. Nevertheless, dreams linked with clarity do exist for everyone. Everyone has innate clarity.

M: When do babies begin dreaming? Does their dream content reflect previous lives as well as *pagchag*?

N: Yes, we say babies have more dreams that arise from the

impressions of previous lives. A small child can more easily remember events from a previous life; his or her clarity is less obstructed. Slowly this changes as the child grows up and the tensions and attachments of ordinary life are created.

M: Would you suggest that parents who are practitioners teach their children dream yoga at an early age and encourage them to develop their dreams?

N: I don't think so. It's not so easy for children.

M: Is there a particular age when babies start to dream? Or is it something that starts immediately from birth?

N: I think they dream almost immediately.

M: There are occasions when we have a dream in which we are receiving advice that seems logical. Are we really getting advice?

N: Yes, there are again two possibilities. If your dream is linked with clarity, you can really receive advice and truly useful information. On the other hand, if you have very strong tensions or attachments, you might also receive advice in a dream, but you wouldn't say that this is perfect advice.

M: Can you give us an example of a specific dream you had that was linked with clarity?

N: Yes. Many years ago I had a friend in Italy. She was a good friend, a talented singer, and she was also interested in practice. This was not true of her family. Anyway, one night I dreamed that I was driving a car to Naples. Then I saw a red car heading toward me. When I looked closely, I recognized the driver—it was my friend, and she seemed angry. I turned my car around and headed back to Rome and, after a short time, arrived in front of my building. My friend arrived a short time later. She no longer seemed angry, but instead said, "I want to thank you for your help." In my dream I gave her a watch from Switzerland. Then I looked at her again, and she had no head. I was very surprised. I awoke feeling very strange. I tried to call her home, but her mother answered and said she had gone to Lugano, Switzerland. I asked her mother to give her the message to call me, but I didn't hear anything, so I called again. Her mother told me that she had returned briefly from Lugano and then had gone off to Yugoslavia on a singing engagement. Her mother hadn't given her the message because she didn't approve of our friendship. When she returned from Yugoslavia, she left again, this time for Naples. On the road, she had a fatal car accident. This is an example.

M: Rinpoche, you had dreams in which you remembered a particular book of teachings. How does this work?

N: Such a dream is also a dream linked with clarity. In this type of dream, one can do many things, such as study, read, or learn.

M: Can you give us some examples of dream symbols that Tibetans believe are important?

N: I will give you two possible interpretations of the same dream. If you are doing some purification practice, to dream that you are washing or taking a bath would be positive. It would indicate that your purification is succeeding and that you are developing your clarity.

If you are not practicing meditation and you have a dream like this, we would say watch out, for it might indicate that you are in danger of losing your money or wealth.

M: You have implied that when clarity develops in dreams, sometimes one can predict the future. Do you have any examples of this in your experience with your own dreams or those of your teachers?

N: If you develop your clarity, you can certainly have these types of manifestations within dreams. Through these you may sometimes discover something about the future. Dreams of clarity are linked with our innate wisdom and the karmic seeds we have created through our experience with meditation practice and the positive actions we perform within our life. With regards to the karmic seeds we have accumulated, there is also the possibility that these potentials may become manifest.

These potentials may become manifest when there are secondary conditions[3] to ripen them. With the proper secondary conditions, manifestations such as dreams of the future may occur. We find many examples of these manifestations in the biographies of meditation masters.

We ourselves can also have dreams like this, dreams that enable us to see or understand something. That is an aspect of a dream of clarity. For example, many years ago, in 1960, when I had been in Italy for only about one year, I had a dream where I was talking to someone, but I did not know who it was. This someone explained to me how the political situation would be after some time.

I was told that China and Russia would have concrete problems. I replied in the dream that this was impossible, because I knew that these two countries had a deep relationship—they both shared the same Communist point of view. When I had been in China, there was a Soviet Association that collaborated with the Chinese in publicity and Communist education.

Thus I thought it was impossible that China and Russia would have problems. Still, the voice told me that there would be conflict between the two countries. It went on to say that not only will the Soviet Union and China have problems, but there will be friendship between the United States and China. I responded that this was impossible.

The voice said, nevertheless, that it would happen because the situation between China and the United States is of a different nature than the relationship between the Soviet Union and China. The United States and China are both interested in business and commercial exchange. They have no problems arising from sharing a border, unlike China and the Soviet Union, because the United States and China are very far from one another. This was one of my dreams. The next day I recounted this dream to my collaborator, Geshe Jampel Senge. He thought that this dream sounded very unlikely.

After a few months, we saw newspapers stating that China and the Soviet Union had serious problems. My friend the Geshe was very surprised. Later he was even more surprised when the United States and China developed a better relationship. This dream is an example of a dream through clarity; the dream is proven in a real situation.

A principal way for practitioners to develop clarity in dreams is to succeed in doing the practice of natural light. Through this, dream awareness will come. But not only awareness. By doing this practice, we continue to develop dreams of clarity and diminish our ordinary dreams of *pagchag*. Through developing dreams of clarity, awareness of dreams develops.

Thus, one may use many methods of practice within the Dream State. There are many techniques of practice we cannot easily employ during the daytime because we have limitations on a physical level. Even if we have a good idea of how to do these techniques, they are still not so easy to apply. In dream time, however, we have no functioning of our sense organs, so we are not limited by the material body and thus can more easily apply many methods.

Through the experience of practice in the Dream State, we can have a very strong experience and understanding of the dreamlike nature of daily life. In this way, we diminish our attachments and our tensions and can truly understand what Buddha Shakyamuni meant when he said that everything is unreal and like an illusion or a dream. The result, the diminishing of attachment, is due to attachment being based on a strong belief that the phenomena of this life are important and real.

M: One time I had a dream in which I received a ticket from the police for parking in the wrong place. I remembered the dream the next day and decided to be very careful. I made a point of putting money in the meter so that I would not get a ticket. As I walked around, I kept aware of the time so that I knew when to return to my car. However, when I got back to my car it was one minute after the meter had expired, and I found a ticket exactly as I had seen in my dream. I had tried very hard to avoid this consequence. Is it possible to change the outcome of a sequence of events after having dreamed them a certain way?

N: Sometimes you can collaborate with your dream of clarity. It can become very useful for you in overcoming many problems. But changing events is not so easy because everything is linked with secondary causes. Sometimes they are very complicated secondary causes, and you cannot do very much. I told you the story of one of my friends in Italy. I had a very complicated dream about her, but I could not do anything. That is an example. Nevertheless, sometimes when we know that a dream says something about the future, we can modify our plans to avert a potential problem.

Once, when I was preparing to go to China on my second visit, I had many bad dreams night after night. I was disturbed by these dreams and became concerned about traveling to China. Then my wife, Rosa, and son, Yeshe, went to the north of Italy for the holidays. My own plan was to leave for China. However, the day they left to go to the north of Italy, they had a car accident.

That early morning, I had a bad dream that I was driving a car very fast. I was approaching a place where the road ends and tried to stop the car, but I couldn't because I was going so fast. If I were to go ahead, I would fall off of a cliff. I did not know what to do and was very frightened. At that moment I recognized that I was dreaming and that the situation was unreal. Immediately I thought, "I must transform." Instantly I transformed the car into a horse. I was then riding on the back of a horse, a very big stone horse. I did not fall off the cliff. After I woke up, at breakfast, a student of mine came from Rome to drive me to the airport. I told him about my strange dream the night before and that over the past few nights I had been having bad dreams. Later, before I was to leave, I received a telephone call from northern Italy. I heard that my wife Rosa and Yeshe had been in the accident.

I thought the dream corresponded to only their negative situation, which was not very dangerous. They were in the hospital, but it was not serious. I still intended to go to China, and the next day I was to go to Rome. But that morning I had another negative dream. I half woke up. In this state between dream and wakefulness, someone told me very clearly, "You must not travel." It was very clear. Then I woke up. I had thought someone was really talking, but I discovered the voice was a dream.

I changed my plans and did not travel to China. I don't know what would have happened to me if I had gone that time. It is not easy to know what exactly the problem was. The only thing I could say is that one month later I heard news that in China and Lhasa they had put many people in prison, and some were killed because they were regarded as threats to Communism. I don't know if this was the problem, or if it was perhaps related to the airplane. Sometimes it is possible to overcome ill fate by clarity in dreams; this is very useful.

M: Rinpoche, you have said that at the time of death one can use the awareness developed in the practice of natural light and in Tantric dream practice. I have also heard it said that one's awareness becomes seven times stronger after death. Would you talk about how to liberate oneself at the time of death and how much experience a Westerner must have with lucid dreams to make it likely that he or she can accomplish this liberation? What are your ideas on this?

N: If you have had some dreams of clarity, you can have benefits and possibilities related to the teaching and the path. However, if you are interested in using the practice for liberation after death, then you must have transmission of the method and teachings on this subject in your lifetime.

As an example, let us discuss *shitro*,[4] a part of which is known in the West as *The Tibetan Book of the Dead*. It is a practice related to the peaceful and wrathful manifestations.

When you receive a transmission—a teacher's empowerment of a student to practice a specific method—then, through the power of that transmission, something is connected with your potential, which, until then, is latent as an unmanifest karmic seed. Subsequently, you use your experience of practice in your lifetime. It means you are developing the possibility of the manifestation of your potentials.

A simple example of potential is a mirror. If you look in a mirror, you discover it has infinite potential, beyond limitation. It could be a small mirror, yet even a small mirror can reflect the whole view of a countryside. The reflection is beyond the size of the mirror. Through the reflections you find in the mirror, you can discover its infinite potential; the reflection is very important for discovering that nature.

If, in our lifetime, we receive a transmission, unify the power of that transmission through the power of mantra, and subsequently practice and prepare for the series of wrathful and peaceful manifestations of the *shitro* method that occur in the bardo of the nature of existence (before the ordinary bardo), then we have the possibility of that manifestation. Because we already have done preparation, we have the potential for this specific manifestation, and at the same time, we recognize that it is just our potential, nothing else.

When we recognize this through the transmission and through the method, then we can have real liberation. Liberation means entering into our real nature. No longer are we dependent on thoughts and judgments and conditioned karmic vision.[5]

When practitioners of the night die, they have the possibility of liberation. For those who do not have the capacity to realize at the moment of death in this way, there is a return to the bardo of existence. Such a return means that once again they will be reborn and have the function of the mind and the consciousness of the senses, both very similar to their counterparts within the Dream State. The difference is that, within the Dream State, the functions of our consciousness are not dependent on the material body and its sense organs. For this reason, as explained in Tantrism, we have seven times the amount of clarity in the bardo than we have during our lives.

M: I have read many accounts of people in the West who have had lucid dream experiences. They can transform a nightmare into a peaceful situation or can overcome their fear in a dream. If they have never heard of the practices of Tantra and Dzogchen but have had experiences of lucidity and know enough to transform their negative dreams into positive circumstances, could they, in the bardo of existence, transform a wrathful manifestation into a positive one and achieve at least a favorable rebirth, if not complete liberation?

N: If one has the experience of transforming a bad situation into a peaceful situation in a dream, it only means that one has this experience in the dream. When one has the capacity of transforming bad into good or peaceful within a dream, it doesn't mean one also has that capacity in the bardo after death.

If you want to be liberated, you must have the power to connect with the awareness of your real nature. Your real nature is not a dualistic vision. Ideas of good and bad are linked with perception, which is itself the result of our karma. Having knowledge of the bardo is another situation. First you need a method to discover your potential, then you discover that your potential is beyond life and death and beyond the limitations of your ordinary vision of good and bad. If you don't have this understanding of your real nature, I don't think there is a possibility of liberating yourself in the bardo.

M: This brings us to the methods of Dzogchen, knowing one's true nature through direct transmission, and the practice of dream and natural light. Can you say something about the practices of Dzogchen and how one receives transmission? How do Dzogchen practices lead to the capacity to liberate oneself at the time of death or even to have experiences of clarity in the time of life? What is the relationship between all of the dream practices and all that we have talked about in terms of Dzogchen, that is, between the practices of the night and the awareness of *rigpa* during the day?

N: The principle in Dzogchen teachings is knowledge. We need to understand our real condition. We can know this only through knowledge of our existence. For example, we say mind is one of our three existences—body, speech, and mind. It is also the root of the three existences. When we speak of mind, we mean mind as a relative condition, with which we think and judge. We are going deeper when we say nature of mind. But there is no way to discover nature of mind if we don't know what the mind is.

The mind is part of our relative condition, our existence of body, speech, and mind. When we discover the knowledge of our real condition in the Dzogchen teachings, we call it "the state of *rigpa*," or "being in our real nature." This knowledge is the root of the practice of dreams also.

Dreams are a part of our life. In our life we have daytime and nighttime. In the nighttime we have confusion in our dreams. In the daytime we have confusion within our mind—judging, thinking, creating many things. This is how we pass our life. Being aware or continuing our awareness in dream time means maintaining the same awareness we have during the daytime. If we have no capacity to be in the state of *rigpa*, the state of real knowledge, in the daytime with practice of contemplation, we cannot have it in the nighttime either. It is the same principle. If we have this knowledge of *rigpa* in the daytime with many experiences, then when we use this knowledge in the nighttime, it will be easier to be in this state. We can have more experiences in dream time than daytime. So this is the relationship of practice to night experience.

M: Is it the same for Tantra?

N: Yes, in Tantra it is more or less the same as in Dzogchen.

M: I have heard that it is essential to have transmission from a master to receive these practices, to understand them, to develop them. Must you also have a transmission from a master in order to develop the practices of dream awareness? It seems many people in the West have had experiences with lucid dreaming. What is the relationship between transmission and developing lucidity within the Dream State? How essential is it?

N: If you want to have only a limited experience of dreams, to have awareness in dream time, or even some clarity experiences, you can do so even if you receive no transmission. However, if you want to consider the dream experience as your path, to see how it affects you beyond your life, after death, and to use your dream practice to prepare for the bardo, then you must get transmission. Otherwise you cannot go beyond and have the possibility of using different methods of practice.

People can eventually discover the meaning of a teaching even if, at the moment of transmission, they do not understand. You need transmission for awareness. Awareness is related to our clarity and our energy. If you have a transmission, there is a continuity, a possibility of repetition. For example, if you have had the transmission for *shitro* practice during your lifetime, you have the possibility of its manifestation in the bardo.

M: If you read about these dream practices in a book, could you practice even without transmission?

N: It depends. One person can have some results while someone else has none. There is no guarantee. But if you follow the transmission the precise way, you can have many experiences.

M: So transmission itself does not lessen one's karma or create merit?

N: Everything is relative.

M: Rinpoche, there is a Dzogchen text by Mipham that explains the practice of awareness and contemplation. How can one deeply understand this text and apply it day and night?

N: When you read a book, you can understand all the concepts in an intellectual way. If you receive a transmission from a teacher, you can have a different taste.

M: Rinpoche, you seem to have a more informal method of transmission than many other lamas.

N: That is not my invention. This is the tradition of Dzogchen teachings. In Dzogchen there is a way to transmit. Analogously, a philosophy teacher, through the language of philosophy, transmits understanding and knowledge. This method works for people who are conditioned for it. People who are conditioned by the method of Tantra can receive transmission through ceremony. Simple people can receive a transmission through talking, like two people, two friends, together. This too is a way of transmission and understanding. The point is that one must experience real knowledge. Without that, one may receive hundreds of initiations and explanations, but they don't account for very much in the Dzogchen view.

M. Is it important to be aware that you are receiving a transmission?

N: It depends on who it is that receives the transmission. If someone is really prepared and has the capacity to receive transmission, then any way a teacher transmits could be very useful, and the person would benefit. If one is not prepared and has no capacity, then it is not easy to receive the transmission.

M: If someone receives transmission but does not immediately understand, is there still a great value in receiving it, or is the value only in the understanding?

N: If someone receives a transmission but does not understand, then at the moment there is not very much benefit. When you receive a transmission and you wake up, really getting into a state of knowledge, then there will be benefits.

M: In the West, there is at least one tradition that believes that all elements of a dream represent aspects or projections of the dreamer. They might ask a person to dramatize each element in order to gain information about the dreamer. What do you think about this?

N: We must distinguish between the dreams that originate from *pagchag* and those that arise from clarity. If they are dreams originating from daily impressions, you can certainly learn about the dreamer's condition in the manner you describe. If the dreams originate in clarity, it is a different case; they are not only a projection.

M: What is the significance of walking or talking in one's sleep?

N: If people are sleeping very deeply and they have a dream associated with *pagchag*, their preoccupations, they feel it is real and very concrete. They are very integrated with this condition. That's why they not only dream but also talk and walk. If you are really angry in a dream, you might also jump.

M: Sometimes it seems as if dreams are occurring in fast motion. Why does this occur?

N: There are two reasons. One is that in general our minds have no limitation. The mind functions very quickly. Sometimes in a very short time we can dream the actions of an entire day. Another is that dreams may be associated with agitation, and when we are agitated the dream becomes fast.

M: Is there any link between dreams and putting information into our memory?

N: It is possible to learn and even train yourself within the dream if you are aware.

M: When one sleeps in the clear light, is there still dreaming?

N: If you sleep in the clear light, then your dreams become more linked with clarity and much less linked with *pagchag*. Your dreams become more clear and meaningful.

M: What is the difference between our dreaming state and our ordinary waking experience?

N: Waking experience is more concrete and linked with our attachment, whereas dreaming is slightly detached. We use the word *unreal* because in dreams we already have an idea or knowledge of the subject.

M: For a lama or a strong practitioner, is there any difference between dreaming and waking experience in an absolute sense?

N: Maybe if one can integrate one's experience completely, one can find the same principle and the same condition in both states. Then life really is a dream.

M: What relationship does the mayic[6] body, which is discussed in the Six Yogas of Naropa,[7] have to do with dreaming?

N: Dreaming is the principal path for realizing the mayic body. If you have experience of the mayic body, you will easily understand how dreams function.

M: What is the value of developing your mayic body?

N: With a developed mayic body, you have total realization of the unreal.

M: When one develops the capacity for the mayic body, is one able to project this body during the time one is awake as well as during sleep?

N: It is possible because one integrates everything.

M: If one receives a teaching or transmission in a dream, is this as valid as if one were awake and receiving a transmission?

N: If you are really aware in the Dream State, then it has the same value.

M: Would you say that, in general, if you are not lucid in your Dream State when you receive a transmission, then this transmission is not of great value?

N: Sometimes a dream of transmission may indicate a disturbance of *gyalpo*,[8] for example.

M: Recently I had a dream that I was with a lama and he was explaining what another dream I had had meant. Is this a dream of clarity?

N: It depends on what was explained and who was explaining. Such a dream is not always one of clarity. It could also be demons creating problems.

M: How can one distinguish between a dream of real transmission and one that is a disturbance?

N: It depends on your understanding and how you feel. As your clarity develops, you will distinguish. If it is a disturbance, you may feel upset the next day.

M: Can a teacher enter into his or her disciple's dreams?

N: Yes.

M: Are there other unusual things that can occur in dreams or through them?

N: Unusual is a relative term, but I will relate several stories that may be illustrative. Once upon a time, many, many years ago in East Tibet, there was—and still is today—a certain province. There were two families who lived there, and they were related. One of the families had a daughter. Every day she went to a mountain called Gundron.

Gundron is the home of an important guardian of this area. There is a particular rock on this mountain known to be the support of this local guardian. The young daughter went near the rock every day, bringing animals there to roam. When she arrived, she would rest under an overhang of the rock while the animals, the dogs and the sheep, would graze. One day when it was raining, she went under the rock and fell asleep for a long time. In her dream she was near the rock with a young, very strong man. For her it seemed very real even though it was only a dream. They talked together and had sexual contact.

Later she woke up and found her experience to be a dream, but then after a few months, she discovered that she was pregnant. Her parents were very surprised because there were no other men around where they lived. They were very remote from any other families.

After nine months, she gave birth to a very strong baby. He

grew up to be a special man. He was not nice-looking, but physically he was very strong. He built a house constructed of many big trees and became very famous because he was so strong. There was a king of Derge, in East Tibet, during this time, who had a problem with Mongolian invasions. The lord asked all the men of the region to come as soldiers to defend Tibet. The strong man became very famous because he conquered many Mongolian soldiers and later became chief of the province. This story was written in a book that I read about the history and origins of my mother's family. You would like to know if I believe this story? Oh yes. There are many similar family histories in Tibet. Such stories are not so very uncommon in the ancient history of Tibet.

Within the ancient tradition there is frequently reference to the *theurang*. The *theurang* is a type of being, close to a human being but not quite human. *Theurang* belongs to the class of *nyen*.[9] Most local guardians are considered to be from the class of *nyen*. Within the class of *nyen*, there are beings called *masang*, or *theurang*.

These beings are considered close to human. As mentioned, there has been sexual contact between humans and *theurang*, and generations have been formed. In fact, there is another book about the history of the first Tibetan king. He came from East Tibet, from a region called Puwo. According to this account, written by an eleventh-century Dzogchen master, there was a woman who had contact with a *theurang* and had children. One of these children was called Ubera. When the child was growing up, some Bönpo priests did divination and astrological calculations to discover what kind of a child he was because he had extraordinary powers. They were a little afraid of these powers. So they said that this could be a *theurang* child and that he must be taken out of their region or they could have problems. Subsequently, they did rites to draw away the *theurang* and then they sent him outside of

Puwo. Eventually, he arrived in Central Tibet. At this time in Central Tibet there was no king. When the people discovered that the boy had extraordinary power, he was soon appointed the Tibetan king. He was called Pugyal. *Gyal* means "king," and *pu* means "from the region of Puwo." His name is widely known as the name of the first Tibetan king, but most people do not know the source of the name. The history book that I mentioned gives this story and other examples of contact between human beings and *theurang* beings.

The next example occurred quite recently. I decided to go visit the place of the ancient Shang-Shung kings in Tibet. We had been traveling by cars, but just before arriving, we left our cars and arranged to go on by horse and yak. At the place where we stopped were some ancient ruins, far older than the ones destroyed during the Cultural Revolution. We put up our tents amid these ruins. Many ruined structures surrounded us. Nearby was an intriguing heap of earth, and I asked the local people what this place was. They said that in ancient times it was a Bönpo monastery called Shang-Shung Monastery. Since this was a very ancient monastery, no more information was available.

That night I had an interesting dream. In it there was a very nice temple with four doors facing the four directions. I entered through the eastern door. Inside was a gigantic statue of a yogi with three eyes. In his right hand was a *gyaltsen*, a victory flag. In his left hand was a *kapala*,[10] a skull cup. I went very close to the statue and noticed Tibetan writing under the yogi; it read "Trenpa Namkha." Trenpa Namkha was a famous Bönpo master of Shang-Shung. This was not the Trenpa Namkha of Tibet, who was one of Guru Padmasambhava's twenty-five disciples.[11] This was Trenpa Namkha of Shang-Shung, who is from a more ancient time than the other Trenpa Namkha.

In my dream, I left the temple through the western door. Outside were many chortens[12] all around me. Suddenly my vision transformed back to my present vision; again there were only heaps of earth and no chortens.

I wondered what happened. I then turned back to see the temple, only to discover that it had vanished. All that remained were heaps of earth. I was surprised. I thought to myself, "There was once in the past a temple and many chortens here, which only exist as heaps of earth today." In my dream I was aware that this was an experience of clarity. Then I looked west at a heap of earth, the ruin of a chorten. There was a light coming from this chorten, similar to sunlight that reflects off a crystal or piece of glass. As I walked toward the light, it began to diminish. When I reached the chorten, the light had totally vanished, and there was a hole in the chorten. I thought, "There must be something interesting inside this hole," and put my hand inside. It was a very deep hole, and I was able to put my whole arm inside up to my shoulder. Feeling an object inside the hole, I took it out. It was a *garuda*[13] statue from the ancient time of Trenpa Namkha; I was very happy with my find. However, I was aware that I was dreaming throughout this whole event. Then I woke up. It was time to pack our tents, and I forgot my dream.

As people were packing up their horses and yaks, I was filming the ruins. At a certain point, I found myself near the same heap of earth that had been the chorten where I found the *garuda* in my dream. At that moment, I remembered my dream and looked toward the chorten to see if there was any light. Although there was no light, I did see the hole. I put my hand in; it was not as deep as in my dream. I had to dig out the earth, breaking my fingernails in the process. When I had reached in almost up to my shoulder, I felt something. I pulled out this object. It was a metal *garuda*, just as in my dream. It was very old. You can see a photo of it in the film we made of our journey in Tibet.

This event occurred near Mount Kailash[14] in Tibet during

the summer of 1988. It is an example of how a dream relates to something concrete.

m: What are the ultimate results of doing dreamwork?

n: If one is highly advanced, one may cease to dream. If one is moderately advanced, one will come to recognize that one is dreaming. At the least, if one practices, one's dreams will become more clear and positive.

m: Rinpoche, are you always lucid in your dreams?

n: Not always. It depends on the circumstances.

CHAPTER 10

The Buddha No Farther Than One's Palm

The following is a previously untranslated text on the Dzogchen path. In it, the author, the great Nyingma meditation master Mipham Rinpoche (1846-1914), has attempted to point out the "true nature of mind."

The Quintessential Instructions of Mind: The Buddha No Farther Than One's Palm

I.

I bow to Padmasambhava,

And to the glorious Lama who is the emanation of the wisdom
 being Manjushri[1] [and like] all the Buddhas and their sons.

To those desiring [to learn] the meditation [of] recognizing the
 profound meaning of the mind,

I will explain in brief, the beginning path of the pith
 instructions.[2]

It is initially necessary to rely on the quintessential instructions
 of a lama who [has] the experience of realization.

If one does not enter [into the experience of] the lama's
 instructions,

Then all perseverance and effort in meditation is like shooting
 an arrow in the dark.

For this reason, renounce all corrupt and artificial views of
meditation.

The [pith] point is placing [one's awareness] in the
unfabricated, self-settled state;[3] the face of naked wisdom
which is separate from the shell of the mind [i.e., that which
identifies].

[By] recognizing [this wisdom], one reaches the essential point.

The meaning of "abiding from the beginning" is the natural,
unfabricated state.

Having developed an inner conviction that all appearances
are the essence of the Dharmakaya,[4] do not reject [this
knowledge].

[Indulging] in discursive explanations [about the path] is
similar to chasing after a rainbow.

When meditative experiences arise as [the product] of
awareness of the great unfabricated state, it is not
through external focus [but rather] through maintaining
non-activity.[5]

Amazing, [how] one reaches this knowledge!

II.

At the fortunate time of [reaching] the intermediate state,

[One] maintains the unwavering state continuously by
recollection of the self-settled state of "mind-itself."

Just placing in that state is enough.

The unfabricated mind is no other than this.

[If obstructed] by the arising clouds of mental analysis [which
create] a distinction between the subject and object of
meditation,

At that time [recall] the nature of mind which from the
beginning is unfabricated—"mind-itself," vast as the sky.

[By] relaxing, free tightness and dispel grasping at [these
conceptions].

Self-settled knowledge is not thoughts which flow in various
   directions.
It is clear, radiant emptiness that is separate from all mental
   grasping;
Example, symbol, or words cannot describe [this state].
One directly perceives [ultimate] awareness through
   discriminating wisdom.
The state of great, impartial, empty awareness has not moved,
   is not moving, and will not move.
[It is] one's own face which is obscured by the stains of sudden
   conceptions: various delusory meanderings.
How sad!
What will be obtained by grasping after a mirage?
What is the purpose of following after these varied dreams?
What benefit is grasping at space?
By various concepts one turns one's own head around.
Put aside this exhausting meaninglessness and relax into the
   primordial sphere.
The real sky is [knowing] that samsara and nirvana are merely
   an illusory display.
Although there are multifarious displays, view them with one
   taste.
[By being] intimate with meditation, one can immediately
   recollect sky-like awareness,
Which is naked, self-settled, vivid awareness free from
   conception.
[The natural mind] is without knowing or not knowing,
   happiness or anguish.
Bliss arises from [this] totally relaxed state.
At this time, whether going or staying, eating or sleeping, one is
   continuously familiar with the state and all is the path.
[Thus] the meaning of mindfulness is awareness similar to
   the sky. [And even] in the period after [formal] meditation,
   one's conceptions are greatly reduced.

III.

At the fortunate time of the final state,
With regards to the four occasions [of going, staying, eating,
and sleeping],[6]
The habitual imprints, from which all conceptions arise, and
the karmic winds of the mind are transformed.
[One] possesses the capacity of resting back into the city of
unmoving, innate wisdom.
That which is called samsara[7] is mere conceptualization.
The great wisdom is free from all conceptualization.
At this time, whatever arises manifests as completely perfect.
The state of great clear light is continuous—day and night.
It is separate from the delineation of recollection and
non-recollection,
And from deviating from its own place, through recollection of
the all-pervading, basic ground.
At this time, one does not make accomplishment through
effort.
Without exception, the qualities of the paths and grounds:
clairvoyance, compassion, etc., are self-arising,[8]
Increasing like the ripening grass in summer.
Free from apprehension and conceit, liberated from hope and
fear,
It is unborn, unending great happiness, expansive as the sky.
This great yoga is [like] the playful *garuda* in the sky of the
impartial Great Perfection.
Wonderful!
Having relied on the quintessential instructions of a teacher,
The way to manifest this heart-essence wisdom
Is to accomplish the two accumulations [of merit and wisdom][9]
in a vast way like the ocean.
And then, without difficulty, [realization] will be placed in one's
hand.
Amazing!

Accordingly, may all sentient beings, by the virtue of this explanation come to see the youthful Manjushri, who is the compassionate activity of one's own awareness, the supreme teacher, and diamond-essence [the clear-light Dzogpa Chenpo].

Having seen this, in this very life may we attain perfect enlightenment.

Composed by Mipham Jamyang Dorje Rinpoche.[10] Translation by Khenpo Palden Sherab, Khenpo Tsewong Dongyal, Deborah Lockwood, Michael Katz

CHAPTER 11

A Brief Biography of Chögyal Namkhai Norbu

Chögyal Namkhai Norbu was born in East Tibet, on the eighth day of the tenth month of the Earth-Tiger Year (1938). His father was a member of a noble family and an official in the government. When he was two years old, he was recognized by two meditation masters as the reincarnation of Adzom Drugpa. Adzom Drugpa, one of the great Dzogchen masters of the early part of this century, was the disciple of the first Khyentse Rinpoche and also the disciple of Patrul Rinpoche. Both of these illustrious teachers were leaders of the Rimed (Nonsectarian) Movement in nineteenth-century eastern Tibet. Adzom Drugpa became a *tertön*, or discoverer of hidden treasure texts, having received visions directly from the incomparable Jigmed Lingpa (1730-1798) when the former was thirty. Adzom Drugpa subsequently became the master of many contemporary teachers of Dzogchen. Among them was Chögyal Namkhai Norbu's paternal uncle, Togden Ogyen Tendzin, who became Chögyal Namkhai Norbu's first Dzogchen teacher.

When he was eight years old, Chögyal Namkhai Norbu was additionally recognized by both the Sixteenth Karmapa and the then Situ Rinpoche to be a reincarnation of the illustrious Drugpa Kagyu master Ngawang Namgyal (1594-1651), the historical founder of the state of Bhutan.

From the time he was eight years old until he was fourteen,

Chögyal Namkhai Norbu attended monastic college, made retreats, and studied with renowned teachers, including the female master Ayu Khandro (1838-1953). At this time she was already 113 years old and had been in a dark retreat for some fifty-six years. Chögyal Namkhai Norbu received numerous transmissions from her, which he subsequently practiced in intensive retreat.

In 1954, he was invited to visit the People's Republic of China as a representative of Tibetan youth: From 1954, he was an instructor in Tibetan language at the Southwestern University of Minority Nationalities at Chengdu, Sichuan, China. While living in China, he acquired proficiency in the Chinese and Mongolian languages.

When he was seventeen years old, following a vision received in a dream, he returned to his home in Derge and came to meet his root master, Changchub Dorje Rinpoche, who lived in a remote valley to the east. A practicing physician, Changchub Dorje headed a commune consisting entirely of lay practitioners, yogins, and yoginis. From this master, Chögyal Namkhai Norbu received additional initiations into, and transmission of, the essential teaching of Dzogchen. More importantly, according to Chögyal Namkhai Norbu, this master introduced him directly to the experience of Dzogchen. Chögyal Namkhai Norbu remained with him for about six months, often assisting Changchub Dorje Rinpoche in his medical practice and serving as his scribe and secretary.

After this, Chögyal Namkhai Norbu set out on a prolonged pilgrimage to Central Tibet, Nepal, India, and Bhutan. Returning to Derge, the land of his birth, he found that deteriorating political conditions had led to the eruption of violence. Traveling on, first to Central Tibet, he finally emerged in Sikkim. From 1958 to 1960, he lived in Gangtok, Sikkim, employed as an author and editor of Tibetan textbooks for the Development Office of the Government of Sikkim. In 1960, when he was twenty-two years old, at the invitation of Professor Giuseppe Tucci, he went to Italy and resided for several years in Rome.

From 1964 to the present, Chögyal Namkhai Norbu has been

a professor at the Istituto Orientale, University of Naples, where he teaches Tibetan language, Mongolian language, and Tibetan cultural history. He has done extensive research into the historical origins of Tibetan culture, investigating little-known literary sources from the Bönpo tradition. In 1983, Chögyal Namkhai Norbu hosted the first International Convention on Tibetan Medicine, held in Venice, Italy. For the past twenty-five years, Chögyal Namkhai Norbu has informally conducted teaching retreats in various countries. During these retreats, he has given practical instruction on Dzogchen practices in a nonsectarian format, as well as teaching aspects of Tibetan culture, especially Yantra Yoga, Tibetan medicine, and astrology. Chögyal Namkhai Norbu is also the author of more than ten books on Dzogchen meditation, including *The Crystal and the Way of Light* and *The Cycle of Day and Night.*

The above information was largely extracted by John Reynolds from a biography in Tibetan and revised by the editor.

Notes

Editor's Introduction

1. Psychotropic drugs affect the mind, sometimes inducing visions or hallucinations. Used by shamans in native cultures to make contact with the spirit world, these drugs are frequently employed to assist in rituals for healing. Examples of such drugs are peyote and certain types of mushroom and cactus.

2. Chthonic deities were considered to live below the earth and were associated with agriculture and the fertility of the land. They were worshipped by the pre-Greek-speaking people, who were of a matriarchal culture. These deities may be related to the local guardians, whom the Tibetans believe reside in specific locations.

3. Asclepius (called Aesculapius by the Romans) was considered a son of Apollo and was raised by the immortal centaur Chiron in his cave. Asclepius became a great physician and left Chiron's cave to help the people of Greece. As he was a remarkable healer, the Greeks ultimately worshipped him as a god and built temples to honor him. Inside these temples, Asclepius ostensibly put beds for the sick, thus establishing the first hospitals. He walked about with a stick entwined with sacred serpents (the modern symbol for medicine), who were said to know the causes and cures of disease. Sometimes he put his patients to sleep with a "magic draught" and listened to what they said in their dreams. Often their words explained what was causing the ailment, and from this information he could offer a cure. Priests continued to invoke him after his death, and he continued to appear in the dreams of those who were ill, offering them healing advice.

4. *Shaman* is a Siberian term deriving from the classical form of shamanism in North Asia. Through rituals, chanting, drumming, and psychotropic drugs, shamans go into trance for the purposes of healing and divination.

5. From W. D. Ross, trans. and ed., *The Works of Aristotle* (Oxford: Clarendon Press, 1931), Vol. 1, Chapter 1, "De Divinatione Per Somnium," p. 462a.

6. Researchers LaBerge, the late Paul Tholey, as well as dream clinicians (including this book's editor, who has employed dream induction/hypnotic exercises) have sought to develop and compile methods to induce lucid dreaming. These include entering lucid dreaming directly by focusing on naturally occurring hypnogogic imagery that occurs prior to the onset of sleep (see Kelzer, "The Sun and the Shadow," p. 144), and autosuggestion to induce a state in which the dreamer will immediately become lucid upon recognizing incongruities within the Dream State. For example, the editor recently had a dream in which he noticed that both a man and a dog, who had attempted to jump from one roof to another and missed, were falling in a way that was incongruent with the laws of gravity. The awareness of this incongruity sparked a lucid dream.

Other methods include a variety of ways to utilize autosuggestion. Stephen LaBerge (see *Lucid Dreaming*, pp. 48-78) has been particularly active in systematizing these techniques. His mnemonic induction of lucid dreams (MILD) technique entails awakening during the night after dreaming, focusing on the details of the dream, particularly the incongruities, and making a strong suggestion that if an incongruity or dream sign reappears, one will immediately become lucid. In this technique, one holds the intention to become lucid immediately prior to returning to sleep. LaBerge reports that the effectiveness of this technique is enhanced by the simultaneous use of technological devices such as his dreamlight goggles, which flash low-intensity light with the occurrence of the rapid eye movements that characterize the onset of dreaming.

Another technique discussed by various dream researchers, including Paul Tholey, involves state testing. This term refers to the practice of asking oneself if one is dreaming at frequent intervals during the day while concurrently analyzing the situation to verify the answer. The "critical state testing" (*Lucid Dreaming*, p. 58) in many cases subsequently leads to a similar testing process while dreaming, and then to lucidity.

These techniques that attempt to induce lucidity contrast with the practice of natural light found within the Buddhist and Bönpo Dzogchen traditions as discussed by Chögyal Namkhai Norbu, which do not particularly focus on developing lucidity but considers lucidity a natural by-product of the development of awareness and presence.

7. The descriptions of lucid dream experience as awesome and liberating or, alternatively, Kelzer's lucid dream experience of being in prison, which served to remind him of the need to work to attain "that fullness of mental expression to which I aspire," seem to echo themes within Plato's "Allegory of the Cave." In this classic of philosophy, Plato described cave dwellers who have become accustomed to the shadowy, muted reality of life within a cave. The inhabitants are unaware of the possibility of a more vibrant, spectacular reality, and doubt the probability of the sun.

Descriptions of lucid dreams that include an unusual intensity, richness of color, and other sense impressions may suggest a "taste of enlightenment." Perhaps the dreamer has momentarily broken the habitual conditioned modes that typically govern perception, referred to within the allegory as "living within a cave."

8. In addition, there is support for the contention that Freud knew about lucid dreaming and made reference to types of lucid dream experience. See "Introductory Lectures on Psychoanalysis" in *The Standard Edition of the Complete Psychological Works of Sigmund Freud* (New York: Hogarth Press, 1916), Vol. 15, p. 222. This evidence is summarized by Bol Rooksby and Sybe Tenwee in their historical article published in *Lucidity Letter*, 9 (2) 1990.

9. Jung's interest in Buddhism and Eastern philosophy was great enough for him to have written the foreword for the first translation of the classic Tibetan Buddhist Book of the Dead, the *Bardo Thödrol*. Unfortunately, due to mistranslations within the original publication of *The Tibetan Book of the Great Liberation* by Evans-Wentz, Jung never had a clear understanding of the Dzogchen Great Perfection teaching with which the text was concerned. Evans-Wentz's faulty understanding of the Dzogchen subject matter led to his improper translations, such as the "primordially pure nature of mind" being rendered as the "one mind."

Jung subsequently misinterpreted "the one mind" as referring to the unconscious, which it does not. The pure nature of mind was a reference to the pinnacle teaching of Buddhism: Dzogchen. The flavor of Dzogchen practice is later described in this book by Chögyal Namkhai Norbu, and is also described in an original text by the Tibetan meditation master Mipham (1846-1914).

For a thorough discussion of the aforementioned misunderstanding, the reader is referred to the recent retranslation of *The Tibetan Book of the Great Liberation* by John Reynolds (see Bibliography).

10. It is unclear to what extent Jung was influenced in his conception of universal psychic energy by Tantric Buddhist and Taoist theories of internal energy, called *lung* in Tibetan, *prana* in Sanskrit, and corresponding to the *chi* of Taoism.

    Within the Tantric system, *lung*, or internal airs, are said to circulate through internal channels, or meridians, called *tsa*. According to Chögyal Namkhai Norbu and other lamas within the Dzogchen tradition, *lung* may be purified and caused to circulate along specific internal paths. These ends are achieved by elaborate breathing exercises and physical exercises respectively called *tsalung* and *trulkhor*, or *yantra*.

11. It is now clear that there are many so-called primitive peoples with sophisticated ways of interpreting and manipulating dreams. What seems likely is that for thousands of years a few initiates in widely diverse cultures have practiced dream manipulation, lucid dreaming and more, while most of the population—then as now—slept unconsciously.

12. Krippner, S., ed., *Dreamtime and Dreamwork: Decoding the Language of the Night* (Los Angeles: J. P. Tarchen, 1990), Preface to Chapter 5, pp. 171-74.

13. Bönpo/*Yung drung* Bön: The teachings found in the Bönpo school derived from the Buddha Tönpa Shenrab, who appeared in prehistoric times in Central Asia. *Bön* means "teaching," or "dharma," and *yung drung* means "the eternal," or "the indestructible." *Yung drung* is often symbolized by a leftward-spinning swastika. The leftward direction is representative of the matriarchal roots of Tibet (counterclockwise being related to feminine energy, clockwise to masculine). The *yung drung* is a symbol of the indestructibility of the Bön teachings, just as the *dorje* / *vajra* / diamond scepter is the symbol of the Tantric Buddhist teachings. It is important to note that the *yung drung* bears no ideological relation or similarity to the Nazi swastika symbol.

    Yung drung Bön is also known as "New Bön." Lopon Tenzin Namdak distinguishes two stages of the development of Bön. The first stage is the more ancient "Old Bön," or "Primitive Bön," which is similar to North Asian shamanism. The second stage is *Yung drung* Bön, with its roots in the teachings of Buddha Tönpa Shenrab.

14. Tenzin Namdak, who was born in eastern Tibet in 1926, was the chief teacher, or *lopon* (*slob dpon*), of the Bönpo Monastery of Menri (*sMan ri*), before the invasion of the Chinese Communists. At the beginning

of the sixties, he was invited to England together with other Tibetan scholars and collaborated with Professor Snellgrove in the publication of *The Nine Ways of Bön*.

Once he returned to India, he founded the Bönpo community of Dolanji, in the Himachal Pradesh, to reestablish the traditional curriculum of studies and the ritualistic monastic activities. He has recently founded a new monastery in the vicinity of the hill of Swayambhu in Kathmandu.

According to this great scholar and leader of the Bönpo community in exile, Bön, or *Yung drung* Bön, originated in very ancient times in a territory between western Tibet and eastern Persia. The founder was Shenrab Miwoche, who reformed the existing ritual traditions based on practices very similar to the shamanism of northern Asia. According to traditional sources, the era of Shenrab Miwoche goes back to 18,000 years ago. It is interesting to notice that some archeologists speak of the evidence of the existence of religious activities, such as the burial of people with objects, starting 30,000 years before Christ. To this can be added the fact that the archeological remains of Cro-Magnon Man, found in Africa, Europe, and in the territory between Iran and the rest of Asia, go back to 100,000 years before Christ.

15. Dakini (Tib. *khandro*): Kha means "space" or "sky"; *dro* means "to go." Thus the term indicates a sky/space goer. The dakini is understood to be the embodiment of wisdom and is ultimately beyond sexual distinction, but is perceived in female form. There are many classes of dakinis, including wisdom dakinis, who are enlightened. Examples of these are Mandarava, Yeshe Tsogyal, and Vajrayogini.

16. Included later within this book is a series of dreams by Chögyal Namkhai Norbu that he recorded during a pilgrimage to Maratika Cave in Nepal. On the pilgrimage, Chögyal Namkhai Norbu dreamed of a text more than a hundred pages long, which included instructions for advanced meditation practices. Spectacularly creative dreams such as these are subsequently referred to as dreams of clarity.

Chapter 1: The Nature and Classes of Dreams

1. Shakyamuni is the historical Buddha who, born as Prince Siddhartha, renounced his royal birthright upon perceiving the suffering of the world, and attained final enlightenment.

2. Dharmas: The truth and basic realities. Used in the singular to describe the teaching of the Buddha and implicitly the path to enlightenment.

3. Karmic traces: According to the doctrine of karma, all actions are followed by inevitable, but not necessarily immediate, consequences. The term "karmic traces" refers to the "seeds" that exist as unmanifest potentials and ripen when the necessary secondary conditions are present.

4. Chakras: Non-material psychic centers located within the body at specific locations. According to Buddhist metaphysics, major chakras are found at the crown of the head, the throat, the heart, the navel, and the genitals.

5. *Rigpa*: Awareness, or pure presence, of natural self-perfected mind. For additional commentary, see *The Cycle of Day and Night* by Chögyal Namkhai Norbu.

Chapter 2: The Practice of the Night

1. Bardo: literally, "intermediate state." There are six bardos. The first is the bardo of the ordinary waking state (Tib. *skye gnas bar do*). It is the experience of the awake and conscious reality as we know it. The second is the bardo of the Dream State (Tib. *rmi lam bar do*). It is the experience of dream time while sleeping. The third, the meditation bardo (Tib. *bsam gtan bar do*), includes all experience of meditation, from novice meditation to total realization. The fourth, the bardo of the dying process (Tib. *'chi kha'i bar do*), is the process during which the five elements that constitute our body (space, air, water, fire, earth) dissolve into one another. According to *The Tibetan Book of the Dead*, first the element earth, which is yellow in color, dissolves into the water element. The dying person simultaneously sees yellow and feels weak and unable to stand, as though all of his or her surroundings were falling apart. Secondly the element of water dissolves into the element fire. Inwardly the dying person sees white and outwardly feels as though his or her surroundings were flooded with water. At this point the face and throat feel dry and great thirst arises. Thirdly, the element of fire dissolves into the air element. Inwardly the dying person sees red while outwardly his or her surroundings feel hot. The person may feel a burning sensation as the body's heat dissolves. Fourthly, the element of air dissolves into the element of space, or ether. The dying person inwardly sees green and outwardly experiences the surroundings as though they were being destroyed by a ferocious wind and loud thunder. At the fifth stage, the ether dissolves

into consciousness, phenomena become dark, and momentarily consciousness is lost, as in a faint.

The fifth bardo, (*Tib. chos nyid bar do*), the bardo of reality, entails the arising of apparitions and hallucination-like experience as a consequence of one's karmic propensities. Using meditative awareness, the individual has an opportunity to recognize these images in their true, illusory, nature. These hallucinatory visions are similar in nature to the images in dreams.

Hence the capacity for lucid dreaming may be useful for understanding them as illusion. According to *The Tibetan Book of the Dead*, an enlightenment experience is possible if one can maintain the view that the frightening experiences are nothing more than manifestations of one's mind.

The sixth bardo, (Tib. *sidpai bardo*), the bardo of the search for rebirth in samsara, corresponds to the Tibetan Buddhist view of reincarnation. The *sidpai bardo* details the process whereby an individual will be reborn in one of six realms (the god realm, demigod realm, human realm, animal realm, hungry-ghost realm, and the hell realm), depending on karma. In an interesting parallel to psychoanalytic theory, the Tibetan Buddhist tradition asserts that the individual, while still in a mental body, will be sexually attracted to the parent of the opposite sex, and have an aversion to the parent of the same sex. In fact, according to Tibetan Buddhist philosophy, all that the disincarnate being sees are the sexual organs of the parents-to-be. This is perhaps the most basic foundation of what we call the Oedipus complex.

2. Tantra: literally, "continuation," in the sense that although all phenomena are void, nevertheless phenomena continue to manifest. All Tantric methods work with the principle of transforming deluded thought to pure perception. See *The Crystal and the Way of Light*, p. 49. The word *tantra* also refers to the texts within which these methods are described.

3. Mother light: In Dzogchen one practices dream yoga, or the practice of the clear light, at the moment of falling asleep and before the arising of the Dream State. The experience of clear light is known as the "son" experience. If, through correct meditative practice or contemplation, the clear light has been clearly recognized during life, then at death the practitioner once more recognizes and integrates with the "mother" clear light. This is known as the joining of the "son" and the "mother." The mother clear light is the natural, innate luminosity as it appears

in its fullest expression in the after-death state. See John Reynolds, *Self-Liberation Through Seeing with Naked Awareness* (Ithaca: Snow Lion Publications, 2000), p. 153, n. 63.

4. Introduction to natural mind: In the various methods of introducing one's natural mind, the master is assisting the student in developing awareness, also called *rigpa*, or the intrinsic awareness of one's natural state, referring to pure presence.

5. *Lhundrub*: literally, "self-perfection." This refers to one's state, or existence, which is perfect from the beginning as the basis of all manifestation. These manifestations, or reflections, arise spontaneously and are complete within themselves. *Lhundrub* specifically refers to the innate clarity of the self-perfected state.

6. Body of Light: Tibetan, *jalü* (*'ja' lus*). Also known as the "Rainbow Body." Certain realized beings (practitioners of *Longde* and *Menngagde* levels of Dzogchen) achieve the transformation of their ordinary bodies into a Body of Light at the time of death. In this process, the physical body dissolves into its natural state, which is that of clear light. As the elements of the body are purified, they transform from their gross manifestation (body, flesh, bone, etc.) into their pure essence as the five colors: blue, green, white, red, and golden yellow. As the body dissolves into these five colors, a rainbow is formed and all that remains of the physical body are fingernails and hair. Twentieth-century practitioners of Dzogchen who have attained the Rainbow Body include the teachers and family members of Chögyal Namkhai Norbu—for example, his paternal uncle Ogyen Tendzin (Togden).

7. Vajrayogini: A meditational deity in *sambhogakaya* form, representing the feminine aspect of primordial wisdom.

8. Guruyoga: Unification with the mind of the guru (one's master teacher), who is seen as a manifestation of the minds of all enlightened beings. The mind of the guru is considered the same as one's intrinsic awareness. Through the practice of Guruyoga one receives blessings from the guru, thus enabling one to rest in the primordial state. There are elaborate and simple forms of Guruyoga. In Tantra, one finds a more elaborate style, whereas in Dzogchen a simpler version may be practiced.

One of the forms of Guruyoga taught most frequently by Chögyal Namkhai Norbu employs a white ཨ (the Tibetan *A*). The ཨ is visualized in the center of one's body as the union of all one's masters. By sounding *ahh* and feeling the blessings of the teachers, one may enter into a state of union with their enlightened awareness.

9. Vajradhara: A male meditational deity, the form through which Shakyamuni Buddha reveals the teachings of secret mantra.

10. Solar and lunar channels: Within the esoteric *tsa-lung* treatises found in Anuyoga texts of Tibetan Buddhism, there are elaborate explanations of the channels (Tib. *rtsa*) in which internal winds travel. The solar and lunar channels are considered to be located on either side of the central channel (*uma*), which parallels the spinal cord. These solar and lunar channels represent feminine and masculine energies. Their colors—red and white—as well as their placement on the right and left side differ among various Tantras.

11. Ninefold purification breathing: (Tib. *lungro selwa*) A breath exercise performed before a session of meditation (Tib. *tun*), or before practicing Yantra Yoga. In these exercises one visualizes oneself inhaling purified air and exhaling negativities and impurities. It is used as a practice preliminary to meditation to balance the energy and settle the mind.

12. The eight movements: (Tib. *lung sang*) Yogic exercises to purify the *prana*, or breath. The eight movements are described within the Yantra Yoga text, "The Unification of the Solar and Lunar" (Tib. *Trulkhor Nyida Khajor*), written in the eighth century by the master Vairocana. See Chögyal Namkhai Norbu, *Yantra Yoga: The Tibetan Yoga of Movement* (Boulder, CO: Snow Lion, 2008).

13. Agar 35 and Vimala: Tibetan herbal medicines. Agar 35 is made of thirty-five natural ingredients; both Agar 35 and Vimala are taken for insomnia and to balance a disordered wind (*lung*) condition. These preparations can be purchased through the Tibetan Medical and Astrological Institute, Khara Danda Road, Dharamsala, Dist. Kangra, H. P. 1762 15, India.

14. Three humors: *lung* (air, or wind), *tripa* (bile), and *pedken* (phlegm). The correct balance of these three humors is considered essential for health. An imbalance will lead to one of the myriad diseases to which humans are prone.

15. Chögyal Namkhai Norbu, *On Birth and Life: A Treatise on Tibetan Medicine* (Arcidosso, Italy: Shang-Shung Edizioni, 1983).

16. *Thödgal*: After perfectly succeeding with one's practice of *tregchöd*, one practices *thödgal*. *Thödgal* is useless without a perfected practice of *tregchöd* and is hence secret until that time. *Thödgal* is considered the fastest of methods for achieving total realization. *Thödgal* practice brings about the union of vision and emptiness. One continues to develop meditative contemplation through vision until the Rainbow

Body is manifest. See *The Crystal and the Way of Light*, p. 130, and John Reynolds, *Self-Liberation Through Seeing With Naked Awareness*, p. 136, n. 33.

17. *Longde*: One of the three series of Dzogchen teachings. The three series are: *Menngagde*, or essential series; the *Longde*, or the series of space; and the *Semde*, the series of mind. These series of Dzogchen instruction ultimately have the same goal, that of bringing the practitioner into absolute contemplation. The *Longde* series works specifically with symbolic introduction and is widely known for practices that bring one to contemplation through assuming special positions of the body and holding pressure points. See Chögyal Namkhai Norbu, *The Crystal and the Way of Light*, p. 116.

18. Dark retreat (Tib. *mun mtshams*) is often dedicated to high Dzogchen practices called *yangti*, a highly advanced Dzogchen meditation technique practiced in complete darkness. Through the *yangti* practice, an initiate who is already capable of maintaining contemplation may proceed swiftly to total realization.

19. Changchub Dorje: The principal master of Chögyal Namkhai Norbu. Changchub Dorje was a *tertön* and master of Dzogchen. He was the master whom Chögyal Namkhai Norbu credits as having truly introduced him to the state of Dzogchen. He also gave Chögyal Namkhai Norbu transmissions on *Semde*, *Longde*, and *Menngagde*. Though an extraordinary master, Changchub Dorje had a simple lifestyle and dressed in the garb of an ordinary country person. At Nyalagar, in Derge, eastern Tibet, he directed a small community of Dzogchen practitioners. In addition to being a lama, he was an adept physician. People would come from distant places to receive both Dharma teachings and medical consultations. Chögyal Namkhai Norbu acted as his scribe and secretary and assisted him in his medical consultations.

20. *Tregchöd*: Literally "dissolving of tensions." This term refers to the experience of total relaxation. *Tregchöd* is the method of maintaining one's state of *rigpa* throughout all situations. *Tregchöd* is the ability to cut through discursive and dualistic thought at any moment, bringing oneself to pure presence.

21. Jigmed Lingpa (1729-1798): A reincarnation of Vimalamitra, Jigmed Lingpa was a great Nyingmapa Dzogchen Master from Central Tibet. He rediscovered the *Longchen Nyingthig* inspired by a vision of Longchenpa. Jigmed Lingpa also wrote on all subjects such as history, astrology, etc. and inspired the development of the nonsectarian Rimed school of Tibetan Buddhism.

22. The one-hundred-syllable mantra of Vajrasattva: One purifies negative karma and obscurations through recitation of this mantra; it is one of the most renowned within Tibetan Buddhism.

Chapter 3: The Methods of Practicing the Essence of Dreams

1. The root tantra *Dra Thalgyur* says, "To practice the Essence of Dreams there are two things: what to do first and establishing the essential points. What is done first is to train the body, voice, and mind. Depending upon the signs of proficiency, one notices dreams, controls dreams, and recognizes karmic tendencies."

2. *Kumbhaka* breathing pertains to holding the breath in a particular manner so as to assist moving the internal winds into the central channel. Instructions for this breathing are part of the system of Yantra Yoga.

3. Concentration on the six syllables and their purification: The six syllables—*A SU NRI TRI PRE DU*—are each symbolic of a realm of existence, including those of the gods, demigods, humans, animals, hungry ghosts, and hell beings. Karmic tendencies to be reborn in one of these samsaric realms, which originate through improper actions, must be purified. Meditation on the six syllables unites *lung* (*prana*) and mind concentration in order to purify these tendencies. The specific practice of concentration on the syllables employs visualization and mantra directed at specific points of the body where these propensities are believed to concentrate.

Chapter 4: The Illusory Body

1. The root tantra *Dra Thalgyur* says, "One practices with illusory body dreams. Perfecting this, one's physical body manifests like a kind of shadow. And because of this, the body in the bardo is recognized to be oneself."

Chapter 5: The Essential Practice of Clear Light

1. The method to gently hold prana is explained in section 3.2.7.3 on page 51 of Chögyal Namkhai Norbu, *The Precious Vase: Instructions on the Base of Santi Maha Sangha* (Arcidosso, Italy: Shang Shung Edizioni, 1999).

2. "The sleeping position of the lion" means that males lie on the right

side, leaving the left side open. Females lie on the left side, leaving the right side open.

3. Before falling asleep, the practitioner enters the state of contemplation with all senses wide open.

4. The four qualities of the central channel are: straight like the stem of a plant in the banana family, slender as a lotus petal, blue as a cloudless sky, and luminous as a sesame oil lamp. Another method to capture *prana* in the central channel is described in *The Precious Vase*, p. 280, n. 321.

5. "Mother" refers to the experience of a practitioner who is beyond all reference points. "Child" refers to the experience of a practitioner who is still karmically bound to the physical body.

Chapter 6: Dreams of Clarity

1. mKhyen sprul rin po che 'Jigs bral thub bstan chos kyi rgya mtsho (1910-1963), also known as 'Jam dbyangs chos kyi dbang phyug, also known as dPa' bo he ka gling pa, also known as mKhyen brtse yang srid rin po che.

2. sDe dge zul khog sga gling.

3. Grub rje bla ma rin po che Kun dga' dpal ldan (1878-1950), also known as rDzogs chen mkhan rin po che Kun dga' dpal ldan.

4. Ye shes mthong grol is a terma revealed by bsTan gnyis gling pa pad ma tshe dbang rgyal po (1480-1535).

5. Kun bzang dgongs 'dus is a terma revealed by Pad ma gling pa (1450-1521).

6. Rang grol skor gsum is a cycle of three texts by Kun mkhyen Klong chen rab 'byams pa (1308-1363).

7. Pad ma kun bzang rang grol (1890-1973), also known as Thub bstan bshad sgrub rgya mtsho, also known as Rag mgo mchog sprul.

8. This mantra is sung while practitioners integrate everything in total bliss.

9. mNga' bdag nyang ral nyi ma'i 'od zer (1124-1192).

10. Togden Ogyen Tendzin, rTogs ldan o rgyan bstan 'dzin (1893-1959), paternal uncle of Chögyal Namkhai Norbu.

11. Adzom Drugpa, A 'dzom (alt. A 'dzam) 'brug pa 'gro 'dul dpa' bo rdo rje (1842-1924 or 1934).

12. These six syllables represent the six spaces of the Primordial Buddha Samantabhadra. These purified aspects of the six lokas are explained in the Dzogchen Upadesha Tantra Kun tu bzang po klong drug pa'i rgyud.

13. One version of this contemplative Song of the Vajra is presented in the Dzogchen Upadesha Tantra Nyi ma dang zla ba kha sbyor ba chen po gsang ba'i rgyud.
14. Bla ma dgongs 'dus is a large cycle of teachings revealed by Sangye Lingpa, Sangs rgyas gling pa (1340-1396).
15. Drokhe Togden: Gro khe tshang is the family name of Togden Ogyen Tendzin.
16. Byang chub rdo rje (1826-1961).
17. 'Jam dpal bshes gnyen, or Manjushrimitra, the main student of Garab Dorje.
18. Sacred place in South Tibet that is a dimension of goddesses.
19. mDo khams sde dge khro khog rgya bo ri khrod.
20. Cycle of teachings compiled and partly composed by Longchen Rabjampa.
21. One section of the Nyingthig Yazhi.
22. dPal Idan Iha mo, Shridevi.
23. Block print letters.
24. Nyi ma dpal.
25. Name of a meditation cave used by Chögyal Namkhai Norbu in Kham, which was opened by the tertön mChog gyur gling pa (1829-1870).
26. lHa lung dpal gyi rdo rje dbang phyug, a student of Padmasambhava.
27. lHa ma yin 'thabs rtsod 'gyed pa: see p. 249 of Chögyal Namkhai Norbu's The Precious Vase (see Chapter 5, n. 1 above).
28. Nam mkha' ar gtad, sky gazing.
29. dBon stod bshad' grwa was a monastic college attended by Chögyal Namkhai Norbu.
30. mTshan brjod, Reciting the Name [of Manjushri].
31. Khyenrab Chökyi Ödser, mKhan rin po che mKhyen rab chos kyi 'od zer (1901-1960) taught Chögyal Namkhai Norbu at the Wöntöd Lobdra.
32. Tshe dbang phun tshogs.
33. lHa 'brong, a famous Nyingma monastery founded by Grub dbang dpal ldan chos rgyal in the twelfth century.
34. sDe dge dgon chen, a famous monastery.
35. The name of a place near Derge Gönchen.

Chapter 7: The Methods of Transference

1. The three types of transference, or phowa, are thoroughly explained by Chögyal Namkhai Norbu in his 1982 Talks in OZ, California (privately

published, 1988) on pp. 211-19. They are also explained in his book *The Phowa Practice*.

In the Dharmakaya style of transference, the supreme practitioner is in the state of contemplation at the time of death so there is nothing to transfer. In the Sambhogakaya style of transference, the medium practitioner transforms into one's main deity at the moment of death. In the Nirmanakaya style of transference, at the moment of death the lower practitioner transfers consciousness through the central channel out the top of the head into some visualized pure dimension.

2. The root tantra *Dra Thalgyur* says, "The two types of body-voice transference are substantial and insubstantial transference. Substantial transference is a method of practicing with *prana*. Through practice with sound, figure, skill, and interdependent origination, one becomes intimate with individual elements. One achieves it by concentrating body, voice, and mind. Insubstantial transference depends upon the capacity of mind."

Chapter 8: The Pilgrimage to Maratika

1. Mandarava's Cave at Maratika: In northern Nepal, where Chögyal Namkhai Norbu did a retreat in 1984, there are two sacred caves. The larger one is associated with Padmasambhava and the smaller one with Mandarava. In the seventh century, Mandarava, together with Guru Padmasambhava, practiced and attained immortality in this cave, which has consequently become known as the Cave of Long Life.

2. Mahasiddha (Skt.): literally, "Great Adept." *Maha* means "great," while *siddha* is "one who has attained *siddhi*," psychic and spiritual powers. In Tibetan Buddhism there is the example of the Eighty-Four Mahasiddhas who were men and women with supernatural powers. These Tantric practitioners lived in India and Nepal during the eighth century. The legend of the Eighty-Four Mahasiddhas has arrived in the present day with only fifty-four Mahasiddhas remaining, of them four are women.

3. Guru Padmasambhava: from the Sanskrit *padma* (lotus) and *sambhava* (born). An Indian Buddhist master of Tantra and Dzogchen from Oddiyana. He is known as the "lotus born" because of his miraculous birth. Guru Padmasambhava is said to have spontaneously manifested as an eight-year-old boy sitting on a lotus flower in the middle of a lake at Oddiyana. He brought Buddhism to Tibet from India in the eighth century. With his extraordinary powers, Guru Padmasambhava

overcame obstacles that had prevented Buddhism from taking root in Tibetan soil.

4. Mandarava: This Indian princess from Mandi was one of the principal consorts of Padmasambhava. She left the royal life in order to practice the Dharma. She is most renowned for mastering the long-life practice with Padmasambhava. She is invoked in certain Tantric rituals that aim to extend life.

5. *Tertön*: One who discovers a terma, a Dharma text or sacred object that was hidden with the purpose of being discovered at a later date. Termas are believed to be hidden in trees, lakes, the earth, and even the sky.

6. Dzogchen Monastery: In the seventeenth century in Kham (East Tibet), the Dzogchen Monastery was founded by the first Dzogchen Rinpoche, Pema Rigdzin. This became the largest Nyingma monastery. The monastery was considered one of the twenty-five great pilgrimage places in East Tibet. Close by the monastery is a sacred cave of Padmasambhava and three sacred lakes. Many famous scholars of all four schools of Tibetan Buddhism and from the Bön tradition studied at Dzogchen Monastery. These include Patrul Rinpoche and Mipham. In 1959, Dzogchen Monastery was destroyed by the Chinese and has subsequently been rebuilt.

7. *Tsigsum Nedeg: The Three Statements of Garab Dorje.* This text summarizes Dzogchen teachings in three essential points: (1) The direct introduction of the primordial state by teacher to student. (2) The practitioner does not remain in doubt in reference to what the primordial state is. (3) The practitioner continues in the state of primordial awareness until total realization.

8. Garab Dorje: According to traditional Nyingma sources, Garab Dorje lived 166 years after the parinirvana of the Buddha, dated in Tibetan sources as 881 B.C.E. Western scholars say Buddha's dates were about 560-480 B.C.E. It is said that Garab Dorje was immaculately conceived by the nun-princess daughter of a minor king of Oddiyana. This nun had been practicing on an island in the middle of a lake when she had a dream. She dreamt of a handsome, white man holding a crystal vase with mantras engraved on it. This man bestowed initiation on the nun and then, dissolving into light, he entered her body and impregnated her. Sometime after this dream she gave birth to Garab Dorje. According to Nyingma sources, Garab Dorje was the first human Dzogchen master. In his previous life in another dimension, Garab Dorje had received Dzogchen transmission directly from the

sambhogakaya manifestation of Vajrasattva. After being born in the human realm, Garab Dorje immediately remembered these Dzogchen teachings and instructed a class of beings known as dakinis in the sacred land of Oddiyana. He also had human disciples, one of whom was Manjushrimtra, who organized Garab Dorje's teachings into the *Semde, Longde,* and *Menngagde.* For further information on Garab Dorje, see John Reynolds, *The Golden Letters* (Ithaca, NY: Snow Lion Publications, 1997).

9. *Gongter,* "mind terma," a terma discovered in the mind stream of a *tertön,* one who discovers terma.

10. *Namkha:* A method of practice and a ritual object used to balance the five elements of the individual. A *namkha* is made in accordance with one's astrological birth chart. It is formed by eight pieces of wood and five colored pieces of string, each representing a different element: white, metal; green, wood/air; red, fire; yellow, earth; and blue, water. The colored string is wrapped around the wood in a pattern that functions to harmonize one's elements. The *namkhas* are empowered by a master or by a practitioner.

11. Phuwer (*Phu wer*) is the divinity who presides at the ritual cycle of the *Phu wer gshen theg pa,* the first of the nine vehicles in which the Bön teachings are subdivided according to the tradition of the "terma from the South" (*lho gter*).

12. Twenty-fifth day: The twenty-fifth day of the lunar month (Tibetan calendar), when the moon is waning, is known as Dakini Day. Dakini Day is associated with enlightened feminine energy. Therefore, many Tibetan lamas do practices associated with feminine energy at this time. Dakini Day is an auspicious time to do *ganapuja,* Tantric feast offerings.

13. Samaya (Skt.): Although the term *samaya* is often translated as "commitment" and frequently pertains to the commitment to maintain a meditation practice or a vow in a pure way, the dream's meaning of this term is idiosyncratic. In Chögyal Namkhai Norbu's dream, the terms *samaya* and *dharmadhatu* refer to successively deepening levels of relaxation.

14. Contemplation: The primary practice of Dzogchen in which one remains continually in a state of self-liberation. In this state one is beyond all concepts of the ordinary dualistic mind, yet one is fully capable of using the intellect and rational mind. Contemplation does not involve trying to find experiences of calmness or clarity, nor does it involve avoiding distractions. In contemplation, when a thought

arises, it is neither suppressed nor followed, but is spontaneously self-liberated and dissolves. It is this practice of liberating all that arises that a Dzogchen master introduces when he gives explanations on the nature of mind.

15. Dharmadhatu (Skt.): This term normally refers to the ultimate ground of being and the dimension of reality as it is. However, in this dream it refers specifically to the deepest level of relaxation.

16. *Thigle*: There are different definitions of *thigle*. On one level it is defined as something without any corners or angles, a circle or perfect sphere. *Thigle* is also defined as the dimension inside a sphere. *Thigle Chenbo* (Great Sphere), meaning "that which embraces everything," is another term of Dzogchen. *Thigle* can also mean "the essence," like in *nyingthig*, which is an abbreviation of *nyingi thigle*, or "the essence of the heart." In another definition, *thigle* is semen in men and vaginal fluid in women. These are physical vehicles for carrying energy. In terms of Yantra Yoga, *thigle* is defined as the most essential form of the body's subtle energy, also known as *kundalini* in Sanskrit.

17. *Nangwa yiger shar (snang ba yi ger shar)*: The spontaneous arising of letters.

18. Initiation: Initiation, transmission, and empowerment of body, speech, and mind. Human existence is made up of body, speech, and mind. First, there is the dimension of "body," which is the dynamic interrelationship between one's body and the physical environment. There are two different Tibetan terms for "body." *Lu* refers to the gross body of an ordinary human being, whereas *ku* refers to the sublime dimension of form of an enlightened being. Secondly, there is the dimension of our energy known as "speech," which is represented by speech, breath, and psychic energy. Ordinary speech is known as *ngag*, whereas enlightened speech is sung. In the dimension of mind, or mental activity, there is *yid*, ordinary mind, and *thug*, enlightened mind. Through transmission (*gyudpa*) from the master to the disciple, there occurs a potentiation that is communicated on the three levels: material, energetic, and mental. Dzogchen transmission by the master is for the purpose of revealing the true nature of the individual. Empowerment, or *wang*, is a ritual ceremony in which this transmission takes place. Empowerment, especially within Tantric Buddhism, may be extremely elaborate, utilizing symbolic instruments and ceremonies. In Dzogchen, the method of direct introduction, which may be elaborate or non-elaborate, is used to introduce one to the nature of

one's mind. For information on direct introduction, see John Reynolds, *The Golden Letters* (Ithaca, NY: Snow Lion Publications, 1997).

19. Rahula: A principal guardian of the Dzogchen teachings. Rahula manifests in a terrifying and ferocious form. He has extreme power and, if not respected, can cause considerable harm.

20. Mantra: Literally, "mind protector." Mantra is the sounding of sacred syllables. Different mantras have different functions: some are used to stir up and activate one's energy while others create a calming and pacifying effect. Ultimately, the goal of reciting mantra is to help the practitioner to transcend dualistic thought. Many mantras are associated with particular deities, and within Tantric ceremony they are repeated until one has attained the same enlightened qualities as the deity.

21. Mala: In the Buddhist tradition a mala, or rosary, is a string of 108 beads used for counting mantra.

22. Ekajati: Ekajati is the principal guardian of the Dzogchen teachings. Enlightened from the very beginning, Ekajati is a direct emanation (*trulpa*) of primordial wisdom, Samantabhadri, who is the feminine aspect of the primordial Buddha Samantabhadra. As the primordially enlightened one, Samantabhadri, Ekajati has all-knowing wisdom regarding the teachings of Dzogchen. Ekajati visibly manifests in a particularly wrathful form in order to subjugate the very powerful and potentially destructive class of beings called *mamo*. "Ekajati" means "one tuft of hair," which is symbolic of wisdom. What is unique about her physical form is that she is one-eyed, one-toothed, and one-breasted. These features symbolize nondual awareness. As chief protectress of the Dzogchen teachings, she may make contact with a *tertön* or Dzogchen master when the time is ripe to reveal a certain teaching, or terma. Chögyal Namkhai Norbu received an invocation from Ekajati as part of his *gongter* of the Mandarava practice. The sadhana is an invocation within which the practitioner asks that Mandarava clear all obstacles to total realization and provide protection on the path.

23. *Tsedrup Gongdü*, "The Union for Achieving Long Life," the long-life practice Chögyal Namkhai Norbu brought to Maratika. This long-life practice was a terma of the root master of Changchub Dorje, Nyagla Pema Dündul (1816-1872). The practice was originally transmitted directly from Buddha Amitayus to Guru Padmasambhava. Together as consorts, in the sacred cave of Maratika in northern Nepal, Dakini Mandarava and Guru Padmasambhava practiced and mastered

the Union of Primordial Essences, thus attaining immortality. In the eighth century, for the benefit of future generations, Guru Padmasambhava wrote out the practice and placed it as a hidden treasure within a rock in East Tibet. Approximately one thousand years later, in the nineteenth century, Nyagla Pema Dündul rediscovered this "hidden treasure," or terma. For several years he practiced this long-life terma intensively. At his life's end he attained the Rainbow Body of Light. Nyagla Pema Dündul transmitted the practice to Changchub Dorje and Ayu Khandro, both of whom practiced it and subsequently lived unusually long lives, 137 years and 116 years respectively. Chögyal Namkhai Norbu received transmission of this terma from both Changchub Dorje and Ayu Khandro, and presently gives transmission on the practice for the benefit of his students.

Chapter 9: An Interview with Chögyal Namkhai Norbu

1. Oddiyana: The location and existence of this country has long been debated by scholars. It has been variously placed in the Swat valley of Pakistan, Afghanistan, and western Tibet. Oddiyana is the reputed place of origin of both the Anuttara Tantras and the Tantras of Dzogchen, and is considered to be the birthplace of Padmasambhava.

2. ཨ: Chögyal Namkhai Norbu describes practices that utilize the Tibetan syllable ཨ in Chapter Two of this book.

3. Secondary conditions: The way in which primary conditions, or karmic seeds, might interact with secondary conditions to manifest a dream that seems to predict the future is explained below in a fictional example.

Due to misdeeds either within this life or within previous lives, most individuals have debts. These debts are karmic potentials that could result in the individual's injury or death when they are repaid.

In our example, an individual who is a strong practitioner of meditation and who has led a virtuous life takes his car to a mechanic to have the brakes repaired. Neither he nor the mechanic remembers that in a previous life he caused the mechanic personal injury.

Due to the force of the karmic seed, the mechanic unintentionally fails to fully repair the brakes. As the practitioner is driving, he subconsciously registers a subtle squeaking of the brakes. Due to his meditation practice, he generally remembers his dreams vividly, and that evening he dreams that he is in a car accident due to brake failure. The next day he returns his car to the auto shop, and upon further inspection the brake defect is discovered before there is an accident.

In our story, both the subtle cue of the squeaking and the individual's experience in remembering his dreams are secondary conditions that help manifest the dream of what might have occurred. In the case of a very advanced practitioner of meditation, the secondary conditions may fall into the realm of what is ordinarily considered miraculous.

4. *Shitro*, or *Kar gling zhi tro*, a terma of Karma Lingpa. The practice of the fifty-eight wrathful and the forty-two peaceful deities that may arise as visions during the *chönyid bardo*. *Shitro*, which is associated with the dying process, brings clarity to those who practice it and prepares them to overcome obstacles at death. It is also practiced by the living for the benefit of those who have recently died. Ultimately there are six bardos, or "intermediate states," corresponding to experiences from death to rebirth, including the after-death experience, all of which are described within the *Shitro Terma*.

5. Karmic vision: According to the Buddhist theory of karma, our very perception is the result of previous actions that lead to incarnation in a realm where there is a shared "reality." Indeed, the same environment may be perceived differently depending on one's "vision." According to a classic Buddhist example, a river, which to a human being is seen as refreshing, might be viewed as a river of molten lava by a hell dweller, while to a fish it is seen as its very atmosphere.

6. Mayic body: The illusory body, developed through practicing one of the Six Yogas of Naropa and a number of Dzogchen practices. See Chapter Four.

7. The Six Yogas of Naropa: These yogas were compiled by Naropa, a Mahasiddha of the Kagyu tradition, and include the following: The Yoga of Tummo (heat), the Yoga of the Mayic (illusory) Body, the Yoga of Milam (dreams), the Yoga of Light, the Yoga of the Bardo, and the Yoga of Phowa (transference of consciousness).

8. *Gyalpo*: A powerful class of beings who cause obstacles such as illness when provoked. Chögyal Namkhai Norbu mentioned that this class of beings may create confusion within dreams.

9. *Nyen*: nyen belong to the eight powerful classes of beings; they include *masang*, *theurang*, etc.

10. *Kapala*: Ritual container often made from a human skull. The *kapala* is a ritual object from Anuttaratantra. It represents compassion, as the blood of all sentient beings is symbolically carried inside of it.

11. Guru Padmasambhava's twenty-five disciples: The chief Tibetan disciples of the great master Padmasambhava during the time he taught the Dharma in Tibet. Each of the twenty-five disciples took a vow to take future rebirths in human form in order to discover terma for the benefit of future practitioners. It is important to note that not all termas come from Guru Padmasambhava; some also come from Vimalamitra, for example.

12. Chorten (Skt. *stupa*): A monument whose design reflects the stages of the path to enlightenment. The interior of the chorten is often filled with religious relics.

13. *Garuda* (Tib. *khyung*): A mythical bird resembling an eagle. In Tibet the *garuda* represents the fire element. It is also a manifestation of lightning. The *garuda* subdues the class of *nagas* (snake beings). The *garuda* is especially invoked to heal disease provoked by the *nagas*, such as skin diseases and different types of cancer. In the Hindu tradition the *garuda* is half human and half bird and is also the vehicle of the deity Vishnu. The *garuda* is related to the Thunder Bird or Fire Bird in other mythologies.

14. Mt. Kailash: Located in western Tibet, Mount Kailash is the mountain most sacred to Tibetan Buddhists. It is considered an archetypal manifestation of the sacred mountain at the center of the world. It is also highly revered by Bönpos, Hindus, and Jains.

Chapter 10: The Buddha No Farther Than One's Palm

1. Manjushri: The Bodhisattva of Wisdom. According to Buddhist mythology, Manjushri in a previous incarnation was King Amba, who vowed to become a bodhisattva and benefit all sentient beings.

2. Pith instruction: The lama's heart instructions; condensed essential instruction for meditation presented by the lama to his heart disciples.

3. Unfabricated state: The awareness arising at the instant of perception; pure presence arising without correction and uncreated by causes. For additional information, see *The Cycle of Day and Night* by Chögyal Namkhai Norbu.

4. Dharmakaya: *Dharma* means "the whole of existence"; *kaya* means "the dimension of that." The essential ground of being whose essence is clarity and luminosity and within which all phenomena are seen to be empty of inherent existence.

5. Meditative experience arising through non-activity: The meditation of Dzogchen is nonconceptual and only accomplished by the effortless

recognition of one's true unconditioned nature. Activity or efforts to accomplish meditation are contrary to the relaxed presence of Dzogchen practice.

6. Going, staying, eating, or sleeping: The all-inclusive four activities during which a Dzogchen practitioner strives to maintain awareness.

7. Samsara: Cyclic existence, marked by birth, old age, sickness, death, and rebirth. Governed by desire, hatred, and ignorance, sentient beings continue to migrate throughout the six realms of samsara (the realms of the gods, demigods, humans, animals, hungry ghosts, and hell beings) according to their karma.

8. Self-arising qualities: As a natural consequence of Dzogchen meditation, advanced practitioners may develop transcendent qualities such as great wisdom, compassion, clairvoyance, etc.

9. The two accumulations: The accumulation of merit through good deeds and the accumulation of wisdom through contemplation. Though both are important on the path of the Dharma, the Buddha said that if one could maintain the state of contemplation (the accumulation of wisdom) for the time it takes an ant to walk from the tip of one's nose to one's forehead, this would be more beneficial than a lifetime of accumulation of good merit through virtuous action and generosity.

10. Mipham Rinpoche: the famous nineteenth-century Tibetan Buddhist master and scholar, originally a student of Patrul Rinpoche Mipham, who wrote original commentaries on Dzogchen and other important Buddhist scriptures.

Bibliography

Artemidorus, D. *Oneirocritica.* Park Ridge, NJ: Noyes Press, 1975.

Boss, M. *The Analysis of Dreams.* New York: Philosophical Library, 1958.

Castaneda, C. *Journey to Ixtlan.* New York: Simon & Schuster, 1972.

———. *The Teachings of Don Juan.* New York: Simon & Schuster, 1968.

Craig, R. E. "The Realness of Dreams." In R. Russo, ed., *Dreams Are Wiser Than Men.* Berkeley: North Atlantic Books, 1987.

Da Liu. *Tai Chi Chuan and Meditation.* New York: Schocken Books, 1986.

Eliade, M. *Shamanism: Archaic Techniques of Ecstasy.* London: Routledge & Kegan Paul, 1970.

Faraday, A. *The Dream Game.* New York: Harper & Row, 1974.

———. *Dream Power.* New York: Berkley Medallion Books, 1973.

Fossage, J. L., Clemens, & Loew, eds. *Dream Interpretation: A Comprehensive Study.* Revised. New York: P.M.A., 1987.

Freud, S. *The Interpretation of Dreams.* New York: Avon Books, 1965.

———. "Introductory Lectures on Psychoanalysis." In *The Standard Edition of the Complete Psychological Works of Sigmund Freud,* Vol. 15. New York: Hogarth Press, 1916.

Gampopa. *The Jewel Ornament of Liberation.* Trans. Herbert Guenther. Berkeley: Shambhala, 1981.

Garfield, P. *Creative Dreaming.* New York: Ballantine, 1974.

Gendlin, E. *Let Your Body Interpret Your Dreams.* Wilmette, IL: Chiron Publications, 1986.

Grant, J. *Dreamers.* Bath: Ashgrove Press, 1984.

Grossinger, R. "The Dreamwork." In R. Russo, ed., *Dreams Are Wiser Than Men.* Berkeley: North Atlantic Books, 1987.

Gyatrul Rinpoche. *Ancient Wisdom.* Trans. B. Alan Wallace and Sangye Khandro. Ithaca, NY: Snow Lion Publications, 1993.

Hall, C. & Lind, R. *Dream Life and Literature: A Study of Franz Kafka.* Chapel Hill: University of North Carolina Press, 1970.

His Holiness the Dalai Lama. Francisco Varela, ed. *Sleeping, Dreaming, and Dying*. Boston: Wisdom Publications, 1997.

Hobson, J.A. *The Dreaming Brain*. New York: Basic Books, 1988.

Jung, C. *Memories, Dreams, Reflections*. London: Routledge & Kegan Paul, 1963.

Kelzer, K. "The Sun and the Shadow." In R. Russo, ed. *Dreams Are Wiser Than Men*. Berkeley: North Atlantic Books, 1987.

Kongtrul, Jamgon. *The Torch of Certainty*. Trans. Judith Hanson. Boston: Shambhala, 1986.

LaBerge, S. *Lucid Dreaming*. New York: Ballantine Books, 1986.

LaBerge, S. and Rheingold, H. *Exploring the World of Lucid Dreaming*. New York: Ballantine Books, 1990.

Lama Lodö. *Bardo Teachings*. Ithaca: Snow Lion Publications, 1987.

Leakey, R. & Lewin, R. *People of the Lake*. New York: Avon, 1979.

Lincoln, J. *The Dream in Primitive Cultures*. Baltimore: Williams & Wilkins, 1935.

Loewe, M. & Blacker, C. *Oracles and Divination*. Boulder: Shambhala, 1981.

Mass, C. Scott. *The Hypnotic Invention of Dreams*. New York: Wiley, 1967.

McGuire, J. *Night and Day*. New York: Simon & Schuster, 1989.

Mindell, A. *Dreambody*. Boston: Sigo Press, 1982.

——. *Working with the Dream Body*. London: Routledge and Kegan Paul, 1985.

Norbu, Chögyal Namkhai. *The Crystal and the Way of Light*. John Shane, ed. Ithaca, NY: Snow Lion Publications, 2000.

——. *The Cycle of Day and Night*. John Reynolds, ed. Barrytown: Station Hill Press, 1984.

——. *The Little Song of Do as You Please*. Arcidosso, Italy: Shang Shung Edizioni, 1986.

——. *Yantra Yoga*. Oliver Leick, ed. Gleisdorf, Austria: Edition Tsaparang, 1988.

——. *The Phowa Practice*. Adriano Clemente, ed. Arcidosso, Italy: Shang Shung Edizioni, 2000.

Ouspensky, RD. *The Fourth Way*. New York: Vintage Books, 1971.

Perls, F. *In and Out of the Garbage Pail*. Moab, UT: Real People Press, 1969.

Reynolds, John. *Self-Liberation Through Seeing with Naked Awareness*. Ithaca, NY: Snow Lion Publications, 2000.

Saint Denys, H. *Dreams and How to Guide Them*. London, Duckworth, 1982.

Stewart, K. "Dream Theory in Malaya." In C. Tart, ed., *Altered States of Consciousness*. New York: Doubleday, 1971.

Sutton, P. ed. *Dreamings: The Art of Aboriginal Australia*. New York: George Braziller & Asia Society Galleries Publications, 1988.

Tart, Charles, ed. *Altered States of Consciousness*. New York: Wiley Publishers, 1969.

Tulku, T. *Openness Mind*. Berkeley: Dharma Publishing, 1978.

Wangyal, Tenzin. *The Tibetan Yogas of Dream and Sleep*. Ithaca, NY: Snow Lion Publications, 1998.

Internet Sites of Interest

http://www.lucidity.com: Stephen LaBerge's website including techniques that enhance the rate of lucid dreaming and techniques that stabilize lucid dreams.

http://www.asdreams.org: The website of the Association for the Study of Dreams.